I0191251

Does God Evolve?
Bible Stories You've Never Heard Before

Lori Miles

Copyright © 2015 Lori Miles

WhiteOak Publishing

All rights reserved.

ISBN 978-0-692-24296-4

DEDICATION

To David, my mentor, inspiration, and dance partner

God moves in a mysterious way
His wonders to perform;
He plants His footsteps in the sea
And rides upon the storm.
-William Cowper, 1773

CONTENTS

INTRODUCTION

I've always been fascinated by Bible stories. Sometimes wise, often strange, at times completely alien to our own world, and at other times, capable of moving us with real and familiar situations. These tales continue to intrigue and inspire.

In this book I explore a few of my favorites, fleshing out the personalities to make them resonate, and giving characters that have been largely ignored, their due. Women of courage and ingenuity, and men of compassion are brought to the fore. Violence is not ignored, nor are moral highpoints. And most intriguing of all is the character of God. "Does God Evolve" is the question that permeates the book. I hope you find the stories as entertaining, enlightening, and fascinating as I do.

This book is the first in a projected series of three on the evolution of God.

Lori Miles

PROLOGUE: THE PRICE OF GROWING UP: EVE, ADAM, AND THE CURIOSITY TREE

> Let us make mankind in our image, in our likeness, so that they may rule over the fish in the sea and the birds in the sky, over the livestock and all the wild animals, and over all the creatures that move along the ground.
> -Genesis 1:26

> Fill the earth and subdue it. Rule over the fish in the sea and the birds in the sky and over every living creature that moves on the ground.
> -Genesis 1:28

At the heart of Genesis lies a mystery: God's strange ways with his small creatures in the Garden of Eden—Adam, and Eve, and the snake. The outlines of the story are well-known. After planting in the garden's very center, a glorious and magical tree of knowledge, God then sternly warns Adam and Eve that the tree is, however, off limits to them. He does this knowing full well that there is no better way to foster a curiosity than to forbid it. Thus each time the young couple walks abroad in the garden for their daily stroll, their eyes are inexorably drawn to that magical tree—its graceful branches swaying in the breeze, its luscious fruit tempting them with the promise of something called knowledge.

So, we ask: is this merely God's primitive way of testing his children's obedience? If so, why did he choose such a cruel method? Adam and his Eve are essentially little children in the state of their consciousness. They, like children, have no self-control. And how indeed can they know right from wrong before they have actually eaten from the tree and become conscious?

Yet despite forbidding them to eat, God has also given Adam and Eve a special spark, a curiosity-spark, waiting to be ignited by the first fruits of knowledge. No other animal in the garden has this explosive potential. Had God really wanted humans to be passive, empty-headed beings, he would have made them so. To this combustible mix, God has also injected the serpent.

The Serpent Provocateur

And what is the snake doing in the garden? In many cultures the snake is a positive symbol of learning and wisdom. In Greek mythology, for instance, Asclepius, the god of medicine, learns his art by watching one snake heal another through the use of herbs. The staff of Asclepius, entwined with a serpent, has become the symbol for doctors the world over.

Christian theologians would later identify the serpent in Eden with Satan, the devil. Yet there is nothing in Genesis to suggest that the snake is really the devil. That the serpent is wily and more than a bit sly there is no doubt; and probably somewhat arrogant as well, since he is the smartest creature in the garden at this point. But rather than a demon, he is more a catalyst for change. In fact, he is just what is needed to get the first couple to do what the Lord intended them to do all along: grow up.

It is Eve whose thirst for knowledge is the greater and so it is to Eve that the serpent goes. She just needs a little push and the serpent's probing question provides it. Did God really give orders that she and Adam mustn't eat the fruit of the trees he asks?

Just that tree in the middle, Eve points. God told us we will die if we even touch it, much less eat from it. The snake scoffs, "You will not certainly die." Rather, "God knows that when you eat from it your eyes will be opened, and you will be like God, knowing good and evil." Why not have a bite, he urges.

Eve ponders her next move. There is God's warning on one hand and there are the snake's assurances on the other. But does she even understand what death is? Overwhelming everything is Eve's desire to know what knowledge means. Is that such a sin? So she eats and then gives the fruit to her less inquisitive spouse and by then he too is eager to eat.

Knowledge

At first, knowledge proves something of a disappointment what with first having to assemble some rudimentary cover up to hide their nakedness. But heavier lessons are to come as a result of their curiosity. When God discovers what they have done, he castigates them "Have you eaten from the tree that I commanded you not to eat from?" Adam immediately blames his wife, and reminds the Lord that this woman business was His idea. Eve holds the serpent responsible, while the snake, having apparently no other creature in the garden to pass the buck to, seems stuck with the curse and the blame.

If knowledge has not yet given the two a mature sense of owning up to what they've done, it has definitely given them the ability to rationalize and make excuses.

The Lord certainly appears angry as he lists the punishments in store for all involved. But then he gets to what's really bothering him: "Behold, the man is become as one of us, to know good and evil." Isn't this what the snake had told Eve? It is obvious that the Lord feels threatened by human potential. And lest they eat from the tree of life as well and become immortal, this insecure god determines to evict them from paradise. Setting an angel and a sword of flame at Eden's entrance to prevent their return, God drives the man and woman out.

Still, touchingly, like any parent the Lord worries what will befall his offspring. Are they ready for the hardships they will encounter? Do they have the intelligence and the strength of will to survive? To get them started, the nurturing side of God makes his children a good set of clothing.

Interestingly, the solution for the Lord's fearful side is the same as for his enlightened side that wants humans to progress by sending them out into the world. He understands that as beautiful as paradise is, it could only be a temporary stopping place. Now that they have proven they are ready for the rigors of the world by eating the fruit, Eve and Adam must leave this warm and comforting womb if they are ever to change and grow. What they need are challenges, problems to be solved—even sorrows to endure—so that they will appreciate more fully the joys of life.

What miracles will God's creatures proceed to bring forth on their own under their newfound power of curiosity? What wonders will they uncover? God looks forward to humankind's evolution (and His own).

I. DESERT WANDERERS FROM THE EAST
(2000 BC)

Sometime in the second millennium BC, a man who would become known as Abraham, hears God's voice telling him to move to the land of Canaan. Abraham is then living in the town of Haran in Mesopotamia, the area between the Tigris and Euphrates Rivers. But God promises Abraham that in Canaan, a land to the west bordering the Mediterranean Sea, he will be blessed with numerous descendants—as many as there are stars in heaven.

Over the next centuries, Abraham's descendents will live as nomads, desert wanders. They are not yet ready to found towns and cities and settle down to farming. They are mostly sheepherders.

ABRAHAM'S SORROW: THE WAR BETWEEN HIS WIVES HAGAR AND SARAH

Go sleep with my maidservant; perhaps I can
build a family through her.
-Sarah to Abraham (Genesis 16:2)

If a woman in ancient times had little control over her own life, a slave woman had even less. Thus, when Hagar is told by her mistress to expect a night visit from the master, she nods her head obediently. But in fact, Hagar is neither surprised nor displeased by this turn of events.

How Hagar came to be a slave, we do not know, but slavery was the established custom in the ancient world. People became slaves when they were conquered or the poor sold their own children for money. That may seem unconscionable to us, but we cannot use today's standards to judge long ago peoples, particularly when starvation was the alternative. There were even times when men sold themselves into slavery for a more secure life. Some slaves were treated well, some weren't. Occasionally a slave was even freed.

Hagar is an Egyptian who was probably acquired by Abraham and Sarah during their sojourn in Egypt. Was her family poor and found their daughter useful as a commodity?

Hagar's life is not a misery, but neither is it pleasant. Although Abraham is kind, Sarah is extremely hard to please and it is with her mistress that she deals most. No matter what Hagar does, Sarah finds fault, whether it is grinding the meal for bread or making their clothes. But Hagar is no fool and she can imagine why her mistress is so fussy. Sarah is old and childless while she Hagar is young. Many a time has she secretly thought to herself, 'I could give the master a son.' Now as Sarah speaks, Hagar carefully lowers her head to hide her triumphant smile.

Sarah's Reluctant Solution

It was not what Sarah wanted, but what else could she do? When she first became Abraham's wife, she had expected to give him a bevy of children, including many sons and heirs. Yet the years have passed with no babies to show for them. But if she is far past the age of childbearing, her husband is not, old though he might be.

Sarah sits down heavily. It is time to face the subject she has avoided for so long. Dear Abraham, she muses. He could long ago have taken another wife and had children by her, but he had not because he knew how much it would hurt her. Was there ever a husband so good? But now it is time for Sarah to do what Abraham will not: make the decision to have a child by another woman. And the obvious choice is her maidservant Hagar.

She didn't like the girl, although exactly why she couldn't say. Certainly Hagar always did what she was told, silently and well. Even, Sarah had to admit, when she badgered the girl. But there was something about her, the way she held her head, the direct way she met your eyes. She just wasn't the timid creature a servant should be. Of course Hagar had the smooth unwrinkled skin and thick lustrous hair that Sarah no longer had.

Whatever her dislike of the girl, a good servant was hard to come by and there was really nothing specific that Sarah could complain about to her husband. Moreover, Hagar was merely a slave and, should she bear Abraham a son, Sarah would become the mother; Hagar the birth vessel, would simply be ignored and forgotten.

Once she makes up her mind, Sarah broaches the subject with her spouse. If Abraham is at first surprised, he quickly accepts the truth of what his wife is saying. After all, he too has constantly worried about the lack of an heir. Although the Lord has assured him of numerous descendants, so far there are none and Abraham isn't getting any younger. He had been loath to give his beloved wife pain by taking another woman, but now Sarah herself has given him the go ahead, so Abraham can rest easy. As he pictures the comely Hagar, he can admit to himself that Sarah's solution won't be at all difficult to follow.

Battle Lines are Drawn

> When she knew she was pregnant, she began to
> despise her mistress.
> -Genesis 16:4

Sarah soon learns, however, that reality can be far different from an idea. When Hagar reveals she is carrying Abraham's child, the most violent feelings of loathing assault Sarah instead of the happiness she had expected. The joy and pride in her servant's eyes make Sarah sick with envy as she realizes that this child can never be truly hers. Coldly she dismisses the girl and from then on, the tug of war between the two women rages full blast.

Abraham's ecstasy at the news is short-lived, as his wife throws anger and bitterness in his face: Hagar is disobedient, she rails, showing nothing but contempt for her mistress. "You are responsible for the wrong I am suffering" she hurls at her hapless spouse. "I put my servant in your arms, and now that she knows she is pregnant, she despises me. May the Lord judge between you and me."

Are Sarah's charges true? Hagar may indeed regard herself no longer as a slave, but as the second wife, and one moreover, who could do what the first one could not. Perhaps she is disdainful of Sarah and slow to follow her orders, arrogantly assuming that now she can do as she pleases. But if Hagar is guilty of rudeness and insensitivity to her mistress' plight, Sarah will prove guilty of far worse.

And how does Abraham respond to the situation? Not honorably. At first he tries to soothe Sarah and make peace between the women, but his wife will have none of it and eventually Abraham weakly allows that "Your servant is in your hands. Do with her whatever you think best."

Why does Abraham give in so quickly? Doesn't he realize that even if Hagar was disrespectful, to permit the bitterly jealous Sarah the freedom to do as she pleases is the height of irresponsibility? Abraham, who will have the courage to argue with God in the matter of Sodom and Gomorrah, is willing to wash his hands of the affair even if it means putting his own child in danger!

Once given free rein, Sarah so abuses the expectant mother that Hagar can think of nothing but escape. Ignoring the fact that an innocent child is involved, Sarah cruelly drives a pregnant woman away into the wilderness, perhaps to die.

Hagar and the Angel

> Then Sarah mistreated Hagar, and Hagar fled
> from her.
> -Genesis 16:6

The despairing Hagar walks for hours, heedless of where she is or where she is going. Finally, exhausted and hopeless, she collapses, sinking deep into a sleep where she no longer has to worry about her baby or the future. Suddenly Hagar is startled to hear a voice, and opening her eyes she sees a strange figure. Hagar he asks her "Where have you come from, and where are you going?" Not understanding that this is an angel of the Lord, she yet knows that he is no ordinary being.

"I'm running away from my mistress," Hagar answers honestly. The angel's next words seem harsh: you must go back he tells her and submit to Sarah. Yet he also reassures the troubled servant that God will take care of her and "so increase your descendants that they will be too numerous to count."

A comforting warmth is beginning to fill the young woman. "You will have a son," the angel continues. "You shall name him Ishmael, for the Lord has heard your misery." Hagar stares in wonder for she knows that Ishmael means "He hears." She has heard Abraham speak of his god, but until now she had not thought him real or that he had anything to do with her. "You are the God who sees me; I have now seen the One who sees me."

Hagar is calm now, secure in the knowledge that nothing and no one can hurt her or her son. Unafraid, she returns to her mistress much to the relief of Abraham. Even Sarah is momentarily grateful at sight of her maidservant. She could not miss the look in her husband's eyes, the distress and the fear, although he had uttered not one word of reproach.

Sarah's quietness does not last long; she is soon once again letting her feelings get the better of her. But there is a difference for now no matter how sharp and unkind Sarah is Hagar remains serene.

A Son for Abraham

Does Hagar tell Abraham of her encounter with the angel? It would seem so for the Bible tells us that when Hagar gives birth to her son, Abraham names him Ishmael. How could Abraham know to give their son the name that God had designated unless Hagar had told him?

At eighty-six, Abraham is a proud first-time dad, but he has learned to restrain his happiness in his son when in the presence of his wife. Sarah's resentment has not abated and she cannot bear to even look at the new baby. In such a household the child grows up sensing the tension, quiescent for the present, but always ready to erupt.

Ishmael's position is also confusing; while he is his father's son and heir, he is painfully aware that his mother is a mere slave. And what about the woman who has the right to order his mother around—she rarely speaks to him and Hagar has warned him to stay out of Sarah's way.

Perhaps this is why Ishmael grows up to be a rebellious "wild donkey of a man," just as the angel had predicted. Still, the boy adores his father and life is pleasant enough until the Lord finally decides to fulfill the promise that he made to Abraham and Sarah.

Sarah's Triumph

Get rid of that slave woman and her son.
-Sarah to Abraham (Genesis 21:10)

To the couple's amazed happiness, Sarah, at the age of ninety, gives birth to a son, Isaac. With this greatest of joys, it is sad that there could still be no peace between the two women of the house. But while Sarah tolerated the presence of Hagar and Ishmael as long as the boy was Abraham's only son, that restraint is no longer necessary now that Isaac has come. She has only to wait for the right moment and since Ishmael is constantly getting into trouble, it isn't too hard to justify her temper.

On the day that Isaac is weaned, his beaming father gives a grand party. Everyone is enjoying themselves, everyone that is except one person. Glumly Ishmael watches the guests admiring his half-brother. The teenager is well aware what Isaac's existence means for him. No longer is he special, his father's only son.

When Isaac is taken away for a nap, the resentful Ishmael follows, unaware that Sarah is nearby and "Sarah saw that the son whom Hagar the Egyptian had borne to Abraham was mocking." Ishmael was cruelly teasing his defenseless little brother and Sarah needs no further ammunition. She demands that Abraham turn Hagar and Ishmael out of the house "for that slave woman's son will never share in the inheritance with my son Isaac."

Abraham is stunned. He loves Ishmael, despite his wildness, and wants to have both his sons with him. Yet that night Abraham hears God's voice, which counsels him to "listen to whatever Sarah tells you, because it is through Isaac that your offspring will be reckoned." But what about my Ishmael, he agonizes? "I will make the son of the maidservant into a nation also, because he is your offspring."

Is the Lord then telling Abraham to simply send Ishmael and Hagar alone into the wilderness? Abraham believes so for despite the ache in his heart "early the next morning he takes some food and a skin of water and gives them to Hagar. He sets them on her shoulders," and tells her where she will find people to take her in. Frightened though she is, Hagar can almost feel sorry for Abraham as he gropes for words to say to Ishmael. Yet what can he say to the son he is evicting from the only home he has ever known? Abraham is spared when Ishmael refuses to look at his father as he runs out, with Hagar silently following.

Homeless and Hungry

> She went on her way, and wandered into the
> vast deserts of Beersheba.
> -Genesis 21:14 on Hagar

Abraham has told Hagar of the Lord's words and as she and her son begin their journey, she believes that God will protect them now as He did once before. Surely in the end she and Ishmael will be better off away from this house of constant strife.

But it is hard to keep faith, when one has lost the way and the food is gone. Hagar and Ishmael are dying of thirst in the desert of Beersheba. Ishmael, faltering, is crying deliriously for his mother to help him. Gently she lays him down beneath a bush, soothing him and holding back her own tears until the time Ishmael no longer knows she is there. Then she lets go, sobbing, "I cannot watch my boy die," and Hagar walks away where she cannot see him. Sinking to the ground, she closes her eyes and waits for death.

"God heard the boy crying, and the angel of God called to Hagar from heaven and said to her, "What is the matter, Hagar? Do not be afraid; God has heard the boy crying as he lies there. Lift him up and take him by the hand, for I will make him into a great nation." Hagar is afraid she is dreaming, but when she opens her eyes there is a well of water nearby. "So she went and filled the skin with water and gave the boy a drink."

Gradually the two revive, and Hagar knows that the Lord is with her just as she had hoped and that the worst is over. Soon the two will make their way to a settlement of friendly desert people nearby, where they find a new home. Presumably these are an Arab tribe, not Jews (although both are Semitic in origin).

The pain of missing his father remains with Ishmael, as well as the resentment at the way he and his mother were treated. Yet once he settles down, he finds he is well suited to the life here. Learning from the older men, Ishmael becomes a first rate archer. The promise that God made to Abraham, that Ishmael "will be the father of twelve rulers, and I will make him into a great nation," will come to pass. Traditionally both Arabs and Jews consider Arabs as descending from Ishmael.

Reconciliation

After this shunning and eviction of his firstborn, Abraham devotes himself to Sarah and their gentle son Isaac. Sarah is a satisfied woman, now that her mission of becoming a mother has been fulfilled, and she lives in contentment to the ripe age of 127. When she dies, Abraham mourns her, weeping for the woman who had shared his life for so many years. In time, Abraham takes another wife, Keturah. Yet this is not to be the end of the story. For the Midrash, that commentary on the Old Testament contains the following moving end to the tale.

After burying Sarah and then seeing Isaac married safely off to Rebekah, Abraham is very lonely. He misses his wife, and with Isaac focused on his bride, Abraham feels distant from his beloved son. Searching for solace, he reaches out rather tentatively to his firstborn Ishmael, and Ishmael does not fail him. Despite their troubled past and the wrongs put upon him by Abraham, the son forgives his father and embraces him, inviting him to his home to live. Abraham is thankful to have his eldest son in his life once again.

Nevertheless the patriarch's restlessness and melancholy continue. It is Isaac who wisely sees what must be done, to help his father and to right the wrongs of the past. Isaac visits the woman who his own mother had treated so shabbily, Ishmael's mother Hagar, and begs her to meet with Abraham. If Hagar has any lingering bitterness, it dissolves at sight of the father of her son. Their reunion is a joyous one as the family comes full circle. The couple goes on to marry, and we discover that Keturah is actually Hagar! Keturah means incense and Hagar has been given this name because her character has become as beautiful as this fragrant gift.

It is a wonderful story of a family reconciled and made whole. Abraham and Hagar live in peace and contentment, and even go on to have six more children!

GOD AND ABRAHAM ARGUE: ARE THERE TEN GOOD MEN IN SODOM?

> Shall I hide from Abraham what I am about to do?
> -God to Himself (Genesis 18:17)

There are times when the Lord's children appear wiser than him. Take God's discussion with Abraham over Sodom and Gomorrah.

God: Should I Destroy Them? Or Should I Not?

The Lord had looked down upon these cities and decided they were so evil he would obliterate them from the face of the earth. Yet strangely God seems a bit tentative, fearing that Abraham, whom he values and respects, will disapprove of his destructive plans. God even goes so far as to wonder in a somewhat childlike way whether he should "hide from Abraham what I am about to do." This after all is the man whom God has chosen above all others "and all nations on earth will be blessed through him." The Lord trusts Abraham to "direct his children and his household after him to keep the way of the Lord by doing what is right and just." Yet is what God himself contemplates doing right and just?

Once before the Lord had committed wholesale killings with the flood and promised that he would never do so again. Although wiping out a couple of towns is not the same as exterminating almost all of humanity, it is nevertheless a pretty radical solution.

At last God decides to confess to Abraham in a rather roundabout way, declaring that "the outcry against Sodom and Gomorrah is so great and their sin so grievous that I will go down and see if what they have done is as bad as the outcry that has reached me." God seems to be playing a little game here, pretending that He is still undecided about destroying the cities when in reality his mind is made up. But let Abraham believe that God is using responsible judgment and not acting hastily.

Abraham Argues for Justice

Abraham, however, knows his god and sees through the ploy. Disturbed, he approaches the Lord, not mincing words. "Will you sweep away the righteous with the wicked? What if there are fifty righteous people in the city? Will you really sweep it away and not spare the place for the sake of the fifty righteous people in it?" This is unworthy of you, Abraham seems to imply: "Far be it from you to do such a thing—to kill the righteous with the wicked, treating the righteous and the wicked alike. Far be it from you! Will not the Judge of all the earth do right?"

God doesn't take offense and even admires Abraham's outspokenness. "If I find fifty righteous people in the city of Sodom, I will spare the whole place for their sake." Once he has the Lord's agreement, Abraham slyly follows up on his advantage. "Now that I have been so bold as to speak to the Lord, though I am nothing but dust and ashes, what if the number of the righteous is five less than fifty? Will you destroy the whole city because of five people?"

Surely it is not everyday that God gets the chance for such a spirited exchange. "If I find forty-five there," he agrees, "I will not destroy it." The Lord anticipates more and sure enough gets it: "What if only forty are found there?"

God declares: "For the sake of forty, I will not do it." Abraham wonders just how far he can go. "May the Lord not be angry, but let me speak. What if only thirty can be found there?" And God replies: "I will not do it if I find thirty there."

Abraham senses that God is enjoying the bargaining. "Now that I have been so bold as to speak to the Lord, what if only twenty can be found there?" God answers: "For the sake of twenty, I will not destroy it."

At last the patriarch knows he is nearing his limit. "May the Lord not be angry, but let me speak just once more. What if only ten can be found there?" God gives Abraham his last words and then leaves: "For the sake of ten, I will not destroy it."

God Learns a Lesson

Now in the end God does not appear to try very hard at looking for righteous ones and winds up destroying everyone save for Abraham's nephew Lot and Lot's two daughters. Did Abraham then feel his words were wasted? Or did he suspect that God was humoring him all along and never had any intention of letting Abraham's words effect his actions? For the patriarch, it doesn't matter; he had a point to make and he made it. Although God followed his original destructive plan, he still listened to Abraham. The Lord would remember and he would realize that what Abraham had argued for was the right way. With the brains God gave him, Abraham had taught God a moral lesson.

THE TABOO SOURCE OF THE LINEAGE OF KING DAVID: LOT AND HIS DAUGHTERS

He looked down to Sodom and Gomorrah...
and he saw dense smoke rising from the land
like smoke from a furnace.
-Genesis 19:28

When Lot leaves his Uncle Abraham to strike out on his own, he makes one of the worst decisions in the Bible on where to live. Lot settles down in that epitome of wickedness, the city of Sodom. Yet through a complex series of circumstances, his strange choice will prove instrumental in the births of King David and Jesus.

What exactly did the townspeople of Sodom do to earn their reputation? Most people assume it was of a sexual nature, usually homosexuality. But it was more like homosexual rape. No doubt heterosexual rape was rampant as well. The Talmud adds crimes of greed and cruelty. We can assume that Sodom and her evil sister city Gomorrah covered all bases and were guilty of senseless violence and depravity of all kinds.

God is ready to take action. Only Lot and his family are to be spared. But is Lot truly worthy of being saved? Is no one else anywhere in these cities of equal moral fiber? Why has Lot continued to live in such a cesspool? He could be forgiven for not realizing the nature of his neighbors at the beginning, but he's surely known the truth for a good long while now. Yet still he has remained, subjecting his wife and four daughters to possible insults and even danger. Was there something within Lot that was attracted to evil even if he himself did not commit such acts?

The Duties of a Host: Take My Daughters, Please

With the divine decision made, the angels of the Lord descend to warn Lot of the impending catastrophe. Lot sees only two strangers for the angels are disguised as ordinary men; yet sensitive to the rules of hospitality, Lot invites them to his home. "My lords, please turn aside to your servant's house. You can wash your feet and spend the night and then go on your way early in the morning." At first the angels refuse, insisting that they will spend the night in the open air. Perhaps they are testing Lot's worthiness as a host. But so strongly does Lot show his concern that they rest in a secure place, they agree.

As the two accompany Lot to his home, they are carefully observed. By the time dinner is complete, an ugly crowd has gathered outside the house. "And they called unto Lot, and said unto him, where are the men who came in to thee this night? Bring them out unto us, that we may know them."

Lot is terrified, but he surely can't be too surprised at their words. Quickly he runs out, shutting the door behind him to plead with the restless mob, "I pray you, brethren, do not so wickedly." And then this father does something shocking; he offers the bestial throng an enticing replacement prize, "Behold now, I have two daughters which have not known man; let me, I pray you, bring them out unto you, and do ye to them as is good in your eyes: only unto these men do nothing; for therefore came they under the shadow of my roof."

Lot has decided that the duties of a host supersede those of a father and is willing to sacrifice his virgin daughters to probable gang rape rather than risk the same to his guests. What he suggests sounds monstrous, yet to be fair to Lot, he faced a terrible situation. Moreover, the relationship of a host to a guest was considered sacred, a sign in fact of civilization. Whether it was more sacred than the responsibilities of a father to his daughters remains to be seen.

As it turns out, Lot's offer holds little allure for the leering group. Threatening the trembling man to "Get out of our way," they jeer at him as an outsider "This fellow came here as an alien, and now he wants to play the judge! We'll treat you worse than them." Surging forward, they get ready to break the door down, when the angels reach outside and drag Lot back into safety. The horde soon finds they have tangled with the wrong people for suddenly they are struck with blindness "so that they could not find the door."

Flee for your lives!

God's messengers now reveal their true identities. "Do you have anyone else here—sons-in-law, sons or daughters, or anyone else in the city who belongs to you? Get them out of here, because we are going to destroy this place. The outcry to the Lord against its people is so great that he has sent us to destroy it."

Lot now knows the fate in store for Sodom and rushes to the home of his other two daughters. "Hurry and get out of this place," he gasps, "because the Lord is about to destroy the city." His sons-in-law look at him disbelievingly, thinking it all a joke or that their father-in-law has been tippling at the wine bottle again. Indeed why should they believe this preposterous story, since they have not met the angels or witnessed the blinding of the would-be attackers.

Did Lot try hard enough to convince these sons-in-law of his before he leaves? And what kind of men were they, good or evil? If evil why did Lot choose them as husbands for his daughters? And if they were good, did they deserve to die along with their wives? The angels have gone out of their way to save Lot, but why did they trust in a weak man's abilities to save his other daughters and their husbands?

Dawn is approaching and the angels order Lot and his family to get out now. "Hurry! Take your wife and your two daughters who are here, or you will be swept away when the city is punished." Still Lot hesitates until "the men grasp his hand and the hands of his wife and of his two daughters and firmly lead them out of the city."

When they are free of the town, one angel gives a stern last minute warning, "Flee for your lives! Don't look back, and don't stop anywhere in the plain! Flee to the mountains or you will be swept away!"

Mrs. Lot: Looking Back

But Lot's wife looked back, and she became a pillar of salt.
-Genesis 19:26

Perhaps the saddest figure in the whole story is that of Lot's nameless wife. Did she have any say in where they lived or was she just forced to go along with her husband's propensities? Trying to ignore the unpleasantness surrounding her, she devotes herself to her children. How must she feel when she hears her husband offering to give her own children into the hands of a monstrous crowd? Oh the relief when her daughters remain safe, and she weeps for joy when her husband goes to bring back their older girls.

But Lot returns alone, stunning his wife with his failure. She fervently tells herself that the angels are mistaken and that nothing will befall the city. As they rush out, "hurry, hurry" alternates in her mind with pictures of her daughters. Then suddenly ominous sounds reach her as "the Lord rains down burning sulfur on Sodom and Gomorrah." The air is thick with the screams of the dying. And Lot's wife stops running. How can she resist turning around when those screams may include those of her children? Can she catch one last glimpse of them? And in that second "she becomes a pillar of salt."

The story of Lot's wife echoes that of Eurydice in Greek mythology. Orpheus braves the underworld of the dead to take back his beloved wife. And they almost make it. But Orpheus has been warned to not look back, to trust that his love is behind him. Near the end of the journey, Orpheus, like Lot's wife, cannot resist turning his head, and at that moment, Eurydice pays the price and is returned to Hades.

The Daughters: Their Decision

There are only a father and his two daughters now, and they take refuge in a cave. Do they not know that there are other people in the world? Or do they believe that the destruction of Sodom and Gomorrah was just the beginning and that the whole world has been annihilated? Surely Lot must realize that the Lord would not take vengeance against Abraham. But perhaps Lot is silent, lost at the loss of his wife and his home and seemingly unapproachable to his children.

It is the older girl who takes command, broaching the delicate subject to her young sister. "Our father is old, and there is no man around here to lie with us, as is the custom all over the earth." The younger too has been thinking and worrying what will become of them, but her mind has taken it no further. She says nothing at first, her eyes widening at her big sister's bluntness, "Let's get our father to drink wine and then lie with him and preserve our family line through our father."

As repugnant as this solution sounds to us, incest was common in those days. In a sparsely populated world, reproduction was essential, and if no one else was available, than close family members mated with each other. In royal families like the Egyptian, only a sibling, in fact, was considered worthy of marriage with the king. And if a sister wasn't available then occasionally a father married a daughter. Abraham comments at one point on his relationship with Sarah: "She really is my sister, the daughter of my father though not of my mother; and she became my wife" (Genesis 20:12). Not until Leviticus (18:6-18) were incestuous practices banned.

For the daughters of Lot who believed that they were indeed the only ones left on earth, their solution takes on a certain sensibility. The older waits until the younger slowly nods her head.

"That night they got their father to drink wine, and the older daughter went in and lay with him. He was not aware of it when she lay down or when she got up."

The next evening it is once again the eldest who takes control. "Last night I lay with my father. Let's get him to drink wine again tonight, and you go in and lie with him so we can preserve our family line through our father." Once more they ply Lot with wine and "the younger daughter went and lay with him. Again he was not aware of it when she lay down or when she got up."

Both get what they want from those nights: children. The older daughter gives birth to a son she names Moab and the younger a son named Ben-Ammi. What Lot thought of the matter when he was sober, the Bible doesn't say.

But God does not seem to condemn the women and their choices. He not only grants them sons, but Moab is destined to become the ancestor of the Moabites of whom Ruth is one. And it is through Ruth that King David is descended. Since the gospels trace the lineage of Joseph to David, Jesus too is connected to Moab. Thus as strange as it seems, Israel's great king along with Jesus, was descended from an incestuous union.

AN EARLY SAINT: ESAU

> I will pacify him with these gifts I am sending on
> ahead.
> Jacob's fearful thoughts on Esau
> -Genesis 32:20

> But Esau ran to meet Jacob and embraced him;
> he threw his arms around his neck and kissed
> him. And they wept. -Genesis 33:4

Esau is the forgotten brother, the supposedly dull supporting character to
his brother Jacob's starring role. If he is remembered at all, it is as the oafish
clod who stupidly sells his birthright for a meal. But take another look.
Although there are far fewer words regarding Esau compared to his
brother, those words are some of the most moving and powerful in the
Bible.

Esau the Careless and Jacob the Sneak

> Thus Esau despised his birthright
> -Genesis 25:34

Esau begins his life as one-half of a battling duo in his mother
Rebekah's womb. It is as if he and Jacob are aware, even before they are
born, of the tension between older and younger sons. The older was always
the favored to inherit a greater portion of the property including the
valuable cattle, as well as to become head of the extended family. In a world
of limited resources, this was the best survival tactic for the family and the
community as a whole, but it did not make for harmonious sibling
relationships.

Esau is the firstborn and thus his father's designated heir. From the beginning, however, Esau is scorned as inferior to his brother. While Jacob is smooth of skin, we are told that Esau is red and hairy, symptomatic of a primitive nature - uncultured and none too bright. Following this line, Esau grows into a skillful hunter and a man of the field. Jacob is quiet and cerebral and tends to stick close to home. He even likes to cook.

The brainy Jacob and the brawny Esau may be twins but it is obvious that they have little in common. As many a parent tends to favor one child, so Rebekah prefers Jacob, while Isaac looks to his eldest. Not least does Isaac especially admire his son's hunting skills and much enjoys the game he brings back.

One day Esau comes in after a full day of hunting. Jacob has prepared a tasty vegetarian lentil stew, and his hungry twin looks longingly at it. Now Jacob is a clever fellow and he has resented, since he could remember, his younger son status. Why should Esau be their father's successor when he Jacob is the smarter one, the more deserving one, the one who will make a better paterfamilias? It isn't fair that just because of an accident of birth, he, Jacob, should be relegated to second-best. Jacob is right of course—it isn't fair that Esau should inherit everything, but nor was it any more just for Jacob to inherit it all.

When Esau asks his twin for some food, Jacob, seizing the opportunity, demands, "First sell me your birthright." Now the birthright is Esau's superior share of all of their father's property. But all the shortsighted youth can think about is the delicious aroma in the air. Mockingly he responds, "Look, I'm starving to death. What good is the birthright to me?" Does Esau really mean it? Will he try to back out of it later by claiming it was all a joke? The wily Jacob isn't satisfied until Esau swears an oath to him.

Was Jacob sneaky? Yes he was. But no one forced Esau to give up his birthright. This was the treasure reserved for the eldest son, giving him both wealth and stature. Why did Esau hold his birthright so lightly? Was he simply immature? Whatever the reason, Esau had no one to blame but himself for the loss.

Rebekah the Devious and Isaac the Perplexed

The years pass and Isaac is growing old and blind. He tells his eldest son to bring him some tasty game and then he will give him the blessing intended for the firstborn. This blessing is what will give Esau the right to rule over the family, including his brother.

Now Rebekah had been eavesdropping on this exchange, and it is obvious where Jacob gets his cunning nature from. This is the moment she has been waiting for. Jacob has gotten the birthright, now they must con Isaac into giving the blessing to her favorite child as well. Carefully she schemes, sending Jacob to get her two young goats, and she will prepare a dish exactly the way Isaac likes it. Then Jacob will take it to his father and steal the blessing intended for the firstborn.

Jacob worries that unlike his hairy twin, his smooth skin will give him away. What if Isaac touches him? "I would appear to be tricking him and would bring down a curse on myself rather than a blessing." Notice that Jacob doesn't seem concerned about committing a wrong, but only about being discovered.

Rebekah insists that all will go well, but in case it doesn't "let the curse fall on me." That seems to reassure Jacob and he brings his mother what she needs. Rebekah prepares the meal; then gets some of Esau's clothes for Jacob to wear. Lastly, she takes some of the goatskin and covers her son's hands and neck.

The stage is set. Jacob carries the food in and lays it before his father. The patriarch wonders how he found the game so quickly. The lie comes easily to the young lips: "The Lord your God gave me success." Poor Isaac is confused, hearing the voice of Jacob. "Come near so I can touch you, my son, to know whether you really are my son Esau or not."

Isaac is still perplexed, "The voice is the voice of Jacob, but the hands are the hands of Esau." But when Jacob embraces him and Isaac smells Esau's clothes, he is convinced. And finally Isaac bestows the disputed blessing, giving Jacob dominion over his brother and the family.

"May God give you of heaven's dew
and of earth's richness-
an abundance of grain and new wine.
May nations serve you
and peoples bow down to you.
Be lord over your brothers,
and may the sons of your mother bow down to you.
May those who curse you be cursed
and those who bless you be blessed."

After the blessing, Jacob quickly leaves and his brother Esau comes in from hunting soon after. "My father, he says, "sit up and eat some of my game, so that you may give me your blessing." His puzzled father asks, "Who are you?" And Esau answers: "I am your son, your firstborn, Esau."

The stunned Isaac begins to shake. "Who was it, then, that hunted game and brought it to me? I ate it just before you came and I blessed him-and indeed he will be blessed!" When Esau hears these ominous words, he realizes what his brother has done and cries out. "He has deceived me these two times: He took my birthright, and now he's taken my blessing!"

One must point out here that although Jacob has indeed stolen Esau's blessing with a cruel deception, he did not steal his brother's birthright. Esau is too full of anger and hurt to remember, but the fact is he lost it of his own free will by carelessly selling it to his opportunistic twin

Desperately Esau pleads, "Bless me-me too, my father!" But Isaac is at a loss and reveals the bitter truth to his son. "Your brother came deceitfully and took your blessing." "I have made him lord over you and have made all his relatives his servants, and I have sustained him with grain and new wine."

"Do you have only one blessing, my father," Esau weeps piteously. "Bless me too, my father!" Isaac can only give Esau the sparser blessing of a younger son.

"Your dwelling will be
away from the earth's richness,
away from the dew of heaven above.
You will live by the sword
and you will serve your brother.
But when you grow restless,
you will throw his yoke
from off your neck."

Esau the Vengeful

When Esau leaves, he is devastated. He has been betrayed by his brother and cheated out of his blessing. Does he also realize the part that his mother played in the trickery? Knowing how Rebekah has always loved Jacob best, and that Jacob could not have pulled this stunt off alone, Esau must guess that his mother was instrumental in the plot. He cannot tax her with it, but the bitter knowledge can only add to his misery.

Yet misery isn't alone in his heart. Esau is full of anger—a murderous anger. And as it builds, he mutters aloud: "The days of mourning for my father are near; then I will kill my brother Jacob." Rebekah has obviously been keeping a close watch on her eldest son, and when she hears those menacing words, she quickly sends for Jacob. "Your brother Esau is consoling himself with the thought of killing you." Rebekah orders Jacob to go to her brother Laban in Haran. "When your brother is no longer angry with you and forgets what you did to him, I'll send word for you to come back."

And where is Isaac in all of this? Has he questioned Jacob about the wrong he committed? Does he know that Rebekah planned it all? Perhaps Isaac was never a very strong figure; Rebekah seems to be the dominant one here. Now that he is sick, Isaac is even less willing to get involved in family dramas, less able to reproach his wife or sons. So Isaac just passively ignores the explosive situation.

When Rebekah pretends that Jacob is going away to his uncle to find a wife rather than to escape his brother's wrath, Isaac accepts it. At the same time, the calculating Rebekah manages to get in another dig at Esau to justify Jacob's getting the inheritance and the blessing. Both parents strongly disapprove of Esau's two wives, both of whom are "foreign" Hittite girls. So Rebekah says to her husband, "I'm disgusted with living because of these Hittite women. If Jacob takes a wife from among the women of this land, from Hittite women like these, my life will not be worth living." Isaac readily agrees with his wife and sends Jacob off admonishing him to marry one of his own kind.

Esau knew his parents didn't approve of his wives, but now he realizes the extent of their dislike. We don't actually know anything about Esau's wives, whether they are good, bad, or something in between, only that they are not Hebrews. Esau tries to please his parents now by going to Ishmael, Isaac's older half brother, and marrying Ishmael's daughter Mahalah.

Whether that helps his cause with his parents we don't know. At this point, the story begins to focus exclusively on Jacob and we hear nothing more about Esau until twenty years have passed.

Esau the Wise and Forgiving

Jacob is now a wealthy man with two wives and many children. After long years of working for his uncle, God has let him know that it is time he returned to his own land. But is it safe? He and his brother have had no communication in all this time. Does Esau still hate him and most important, does he want to kill him? Will he seek to hurt Jacob's family? There are so many questions that Jacob does not know the answer to because he knows nothing about his brother. Always at odds, they never sought to understand each other.

Jacob hopes to placate his twin with effusive gifts. He sends one of his men to Esau with a message from "Your servant Jacob" describing all the cattle, and sheep and servants that Jacob has, "that I may find favor in your eyes." But the messenger returns with ominous news. "We went to your brother Esau, and now he is coming to meet you, and four hundred men are with him."

Fearing the worst, Jacob divides his people and all his animals into two groups, hoping that one at least may survive. Then he prepares a magnificent gift that he prays Esau will be impressed with, including 220 goats, 220 sheep, and numerous camels, cows and donkeys. As he sends the gift on ahead, Jacob prays to God to save him and his family from his brother.

Suddenly Jacob looks up and there is Esau approaching with his men. Running ahead, Jacob approaches his brother and bows low to the ground seven times in a gesture of obeisance. He is prepared for anything, anything that is except what his brother actually does.

"Esau runs to meet Jacob and embraces him; he throws his arms around his neck and kisses him." Jacob is expecting a vengeance seeking brother, and instead finds one who is full of love and forgiveness. The two brothers weep, reconciled at last.

What has happened to Esau in the intervening years to give him such wisdom? How did he learn to forgive? We know that he went to his uncle Ishmael and wed his cousin. He could no longer bear to stay at the home of his parents and Ishmael's home was a good refuge. Ishmael after all was also an older son who got pushed away, so to speak, by the younger. Ishmael, like Esau, felt like an outsider, and if anyone could empathize with the anger and loneliness that Esau felt, it was surely his uncle.

Time passes and Esau learns that holding on to anger and the desire for vengeance is useless and self-destructive. He makes peace with the fact that he has lost the birthright and the blessing. He accepts that he himself was partly responsible through his own actions. And he finds he can still earn his own wealth and head his own family. Now he wants nothing more than to become reacquainted with the brother who had been lost to him.

"What do you mean by all these droves I met?" Esau jovially asks his brother. Jacob tells him they are gifts for him "To find favor in your eyes, my lord."

Esau protests that he doesn't need them, but Jacob insists "If I have found favor in your eyes, accept this gift from me. For to see your face is like seeing the face of God, now that you have received me favorably." And to please his brother, Esau accepts.

Esau and his dysfunctional parents, who play favorites, plus the poisonous sibling rivalries, are quite familiar to us today. However, of all the family, Esau is the one who changes, who ultimately matures more than his brother does. Esau is the one who exemplifies the best in the Bible: love and compassion and forgiveness.

Jacob may be the center of the story, but it is Esau, with his generous spirit, who is the unsung hero of the tale.

THE BED TRICK: LABAN, YOUNG JACOB, AND LEAH

Now Laban had two daughters; the name of the
older was Leah, and the name of the younger
was Rachel. And Leah's eyes were weak, but
Rachel was beautiful of form and face.
-Genesis 29:16

The bride was heavily veiled, and no one could see the anxiety etched on
her homely face. Leah might be marrying the man she loved, but her groom
had no idea who he was marrying!

Jacob had no reason to doubt that before the night was over, he would
be wed to his adored cousin Rachel. Wasn't that the deal he had struck with
his Uncle Laban? Seven years he had toiled for the man and then had said
"give me my wife, for my time is completed."

Jacob was not to know the plan percolating in his manipulative relative's
head. For as soon as Laban gave his consent for a marriage to his daughter,
he immediately sent for his older girl Leah. My child, you want to marry
Jacob, don't you, Laban said to her. Leah was stunned. Of course she
wanted to marry her cousin. She had loved him the moment she saw him,
just as Jacob had fallen for the flawless Rachel. And Rachel? Well Rachel
continued to adore Rachel.

But what her father was suggesting was surely impossible. The good-natured Leah had long ago accepted her lot in life: that of the plain daughter always showing to disadvantage next to her radiant younger sister. Yet now her father was telling her that according to tradition, she as the elder must wed first. Why not Jacob? All she had to do was remain silent as a good bride would anyway. As for Rachel, Laban would ensure that she was far away, lest she balk at his plans.

Leah was torn. She knew this was wrong. Yet wouldn't it be equally wrong to disobey her father? Little by little Leah fell in with the plot. And surely, she convinced herself, once she was his wife, Jacob would come to love her.

A Surprise for Jacob

> Laban gathered all the men of the place and made a feast. Now in the evening he took his daughter Leah, and brought her to him; and Jacob went in to her.
> -Genesis 29:22-23

Darkness fell as Leah waited in an outside room for the men to finish their grand celebration—a strictly male affair in ancient times. The bride's part only came later when she was brought to the groom for the wedding night. Leah trembled as the moment of truth approached, certain that Jacob would recognize her awkward gait, her ungainly figure even through the heavy clothes and veil.

She needn't have worried. Laban had seen to it that his new son-in-law was well plied with food and wine. And indeed, the bridegroom was happy and a little tipsy, and saw nothing amiss in the dimness when at last Laban came to his room late that evening escorting his new wife. The eager Jacob certainly didn't notice that she was taller than Rachel for her head was bowed so low—in fear he assumed for the wedding night. And if she made no sound; well that was to be expected from a nervous and virginal young maid. Jacob was determined to be kind and gentle and later flattered himself that his bride had welcomed his embraces. He fell asleep well content.

In the morning with the sun streaming in, the young husband awoke and turned to his bride and "behold, it was Leah!" At the sight of Jacob's angry shock, Leah shivered. Tentatively she reached out to her husband, but ignoring her, he stormed out of the room to Laban, demanding, "What is this you have done to me? Was it not for Rachel that I served with you? Why then have you deceived me?"

His wily uncle was ready. Surely Jacob knew that "it is not the practice in our place to marry off the younger before the firstborn." Ah but if Jacob still wanted to marry Rachel, he could have her too and soon. All he had to do was promise to work for another seven years and Rachel would be his the following week.

Jacob was still, struggling to keep his anger under control, realizing how completely his uncle had duped him. Once upon a time he had thought himself so clever when he deceived his father and brother. Now Jacob realized that when it came to deception, he was a babe compared to his conniving uncle. Perhaps, he admitted, his arrogant self deserved to be so humbled. But someday he promised himself, 'I will get the better of you my uncle.'

A tight smile fixed on his face, Jacob agreed to his uncle's terms. All Laban asked was that he complete his marriage week with Leah and then Rachel was his. So Jacob returned to Leah and she was grateful that he did not hold her responsible for the trick, but accepted that she had to act the obedient daughter. Jacob was kind and generous and in the following days seemed to grow genuinely fond of Leah. The new wife had hopes that her husband was coming to love her.

The Second Wife

> Now the Lord saw that Leah was unloved, and
> He opened her womb.
> -Genesis 29:31

Then the week was up and Leah's idyll came to an end. Laban brought his younger daughter to Jacob as wife. "So Jacob went in to Rachel also, and indeed he loved Rachel more than Leah."

Leah was once again alone, and forced everyday to see the devotion in Jacob's eyes towards his beloved Rachel. But if Leah is a lonely bride, she is soon a hopeful mother-to-be. And when she presents Jacob with his first child, a son named Reuben, once more she tells herself, "Surely now my husband will love me." These sad words are to be Leah's poignant refrain.

RACHEL'S DESPERATE BARGAIN: HER HUSBAND FOR A MANDRAKE ROOT

Now in the days of the wheat harvest Reuben
went and found mandrakes in the field, and
brought them to his mother Leah.
-Genesis 30:14

Even in biblical times, the mandrake was a legendary plant. It's oddly humanlike shape; coupled with its narcotic affects gave rise to a magical aura. Add to that, the eerie "cry" it supposedly made when pulled from the ground and you have the reason why Rachel latched on to the mandrake in her despair.

Once upon a time Rachel had been viewed as the most fortunate of women. She was beautiful, adored by her family and the beloved of her husband Jacob. But all that had changed. Rachel remained childless, while her sister Leah—Jacob's other wife—was a virtual baby machine with four children so far. Lines of bitterness had begun to make inroads on Rachel's lovely face, and she had even lashed out at her husband, "Give me children, or else I die." Jacob was stunned and exploded in a rare burst of anger against his wife, "Am I in the place of God, who has withheld from you the fruit of the womb?"

The memory of Jacob's words still stung in her memory when Rachel caught sight of her young nephew Reuben playing in the fields, a mandrake in his hands. He was showing his mother Leah his strange discovery when Rachel rushed out to meet them. "Please," Rachel smiled brightly at Leah, "give me some of your son's mandrakes."

Leah's eyes narrowed as she looked at her sister and rival. She well knew the mandrake's reputation as a fertility charm and saw no reason why she should help Rachel in her quest. Had her sister ever been the least bit compassionate regarding Leah's unrequited love for their mutual husband? No, she had only caused more complications by giving Jacob her servant girl so that "through her I too may have children." Even if this was an accepted practice, Leah believed Rachel's real aim was to hurt her and prick her pride in the children she had borne Jacob.

Indeed after Bilhah bore Jacob two sons, Rachel was heard to murmur "With mighty wrestlings I have wrestled with my sister, and I have indeed prevailed." Not to be outdone, and even though she already had four sons, Leah gave her maid Zilpah to Jacob as well and when she also had two sons, Leah felt some satisfaction for now Rachel was the only woman in Jacob's household who did not have his child.

Two Sisters, One Plant, and a Night of Love

You must come in to me, for I have surely hired
you with my son's mandrakes.
-Leah to Jacob (Genesis 30:16)

Of course it wasn't Rachel's fault that Jacob didn't love Leah, yet Leah was in no mood to be generous and with poison in her eyes, she denied Rachel's request for the mandrake "Is it a small matter for you to take my husband? And would you take my son's mandrakes also?" Rachel stared at the plant which had now become an obsession. What, she pondered, could she offer Leah to trade? And then it came to her. She knew it had been months since Jacob had paid any attention to Leah. Why not offer her sister a night of love with Jacob? "Therefore he may lie with you tonight in return for your son's mandrakes."

Poor Leah! She was silent for a moment, wanting to throw Rachel's offer in her face. But what did the mandrake matter when she was starved for her husband's affection? Leah nodded to Rachel and when Jacob came in from the fields, Leah went to meet him and told him what was on the evening's schedule. Now although Jacob was no weakling, he seemed to accept whatever sleeping arrangements—remember Bilhah and Zilpah—his wives came up with, including spending this night with Leah as payment. Perhaps by now Jacob was so exhausted by all the bickering in the house that he was willing to do almost anything in the interests of family peace.

So Leah got her night with Jacob and Rachel got the mandrake. Was the mandrake a success? In an ironical way it was for conception did indeed take place. Unfortunately though for Rachel it was Leah who conceived! And even with Jacob's scant attention, Leah conceived twice more after that. Seven children she bore Jacob as the envious Rachel cursed her "shame."

Finally after many years, Rachel began to accept her situation, remembering Sarah and Rebekah before her and the many barren years they had suffered through. If God wanted her to have a child, she realized, she would have one and there was nothing to be done about it. And at long last "God remembered Rachel and God gave heed to her and opened her womb;" and Joseph was born.

TRICKSTER: JACOB'S MAGIC SHEEP-MATING POLES

Laban was a con man. None knew better than Jacob that the affable Laban would take the clothes off your back, and then try to convince you it was for your own good! But Jacob was himself no slouch when it came to trickery and after twenty years of toiling for his father-in-law, he not only had a strategy, he also had an unseen ally: God.

The Game Begins: Stripes, Spots and Black Sheep

> You had little before I came and it has increased
> to a multitude, and the Lord has blessed you
> wherever I turned.
> -Jacob to Laban (Genesis 30:30)

The conversation was friendly enough at first. "Name your wages and I will pay them," Laban had offered when his nephew and son-in-law told him he was thinking of leaving his employ. Jacob thanked him but insisted that soon he must return to his own homeland, and pointedly mentioned how Laban had prospered under the years of his stewardship. "You yourself know how I have served you and how your cattle have fared with me. But now, when shall I provide for my own household also?"

Laban smiled warily and asked Jacob what he wanted. "Nothing," was the surprising answer, nothing except for one small thing, "Let me go through all your flocks today and remove from them every speckled or spotted sheep, every dark-colored lamb and every spotted or speckled goat." Jacob would keep those for himself and those few animals among Laban's vast herd would serve as his wages. "Do this one thing for me, and I will go on tending your flocks and watching over them."

It was easy for Laban to agree, "Let it be as you have said," for he had no intention of fulfilling the bargain. As soon as his nephew had gone, the wily old fox went out with his sons and removed all the goats that were streaked or spotted with white and all the dark-colored lambs and sent them far away. When Jacob went back to the herd, he knew that Laban had cheated him, yet strangely he said nary a word about the missing animals and continued to tend the flocks as usual.

Laban was expecting an angry response from Jacob and he was all prepared to give one of his oily excuses. What he didn't expect was reproductive magic. Taking freshly cut tree branches, Jacob peeled the bark, so that the inner white was exposed, and placed them in the watering holes where the animals came to drink. When the animals mated in front of them, the result was babies with white markings.

Jacob would later say that he got divine instructions in a dream about speckled goats and branches. Cleverly Jacob added a further twist by observing which females were strong and which weak. "Whenever the stronger females were in heat, Jacob would place the branches in the troughs in front of the animals so they would mate near the branches, but if the animals were weak, he would not place them there." As a result, Jacob's flocks were healthy and strong while Laban's were weak and puny.

God and Jacob made a good team. Soon Jacob "grew exceedingly prosperous and came to own large flocks, and maidservants and menservants, and camels and donkeys."

It was inevitable that Laban would hear of Jacob's success. What would he do then? Laban was not a good loser, and certainly not when it came to such riches. Jacob had won the battle but would, he wondered, win the war.

THE MYSTERIOUS CASE OF THE STOLEN PAGAN IDOLS: RACHEL'S THEFT FROM HER FATHER

> Jacob saw the attitude of Laban, and behold, it
> was not friendly toward him as formerly.
> -Genesis 31:2

The family was frantic as Rachel, Leah and their mutual husband Jacob prepared to flee from Laban's household. Jacob's orders had been clear: they were to take only their own belongings and leave anything that was their father's behind. Yet when Rachel's eye caught sight of the teraphim or household gods, she did a very curious thing. Looking about to make sure that no one was looking, she quickly hid these little idols in her clothing.

Days ago, Jacob had summoned his wives for a family conference. He was obviously disturbed and the sisters quickly guessed that their father was once again being his slippery, dishonest self. This time, Jacob gave them to understand, matters had reached a crisis.

"You know that I have served your father with all my strength. Yet your father has cheated me and changed my wages ten times." It was only through God's intervention that Jacob had been protected against Laban's tricks. But as Jacob prospered with his flocks, his father-in-law grew progressively angrier. Laban hated losing and convinced himself that he had been the innocent victim!

Now Jacob must have foreseen that his father-in-law would not easily accept being bested. Yet the extent of the coldness in Laban's eyes and voice stunned him and made him afraid. The easy affection had been replaced by an attitude of menace. Nor was it just Laban that Jacob felt threatened by but his sons. They too had been heard to complain that "Jacob has taken away all that was our father's, and from what belonged to our father he has made all this wealth." They chose not to remember that it was Jacob who had done most of the work over the years.

When Jacob heard the voice of God telling him to "return to the land of your fathers and to your relatives, and I will be with you," it confirmed for Jacob what he already suspected: that it was time to leave his father-in-law's land. Jacob would have to tell Leah and Rachel what was happening and find out where their loyalties lay.

For once the rival sisters were united, as furious at Laban's actions as their husband was. With Rachel's approval, Leah spoke, "Do we still have any portion or inheritance in our father's house? Are we not reckoned by him as foreigners?" Rachel seconded her sister, "For he has sold us, and has also entirely consumed our purchase price. Surely all the wealth which God has taken away from our father belongs to us and our children; now then, do whatever God has said to you."

A Raging Laban Goes in Pursuit

> So he fled with all that he had; and he arose and
> crossed the Euphrates River, and set his face
> toward the hill country of Gilead.
> -Genesis 31:21

Relieved, Jacob assured them that all would be well, but they must leave in secret as soon as Laban was far away. That time arrived when Laban went to shear his flocks, and now everyone was rushing about, from Jacob and Leah to the servants and children, collecting what was theirs. It was then that Rachel committed her larcenous deed. Unaware of his wife's theft, Jacob settled Rachel and Leah and the children upon camels "and drove away all his livestock and all his property which he had gathered."

The journey was a frightening one for the two women as they left their family and the only home they had ever known. The sisters clung to each other as they never had before for who knew what lay before them. They even cried in sorrow for their father, reprobate though he was even as they wondered what he would do should he catch up with them.

Laban was shocked and enraged when he returned home to find Jacob had gotten the better of him. Quickly he went in pursuit of the runaways. On the seventh day Laban overtook them, striding into their camp, self-righteously demanding to know why Jacob had so betrayed him. "What have you done by deceiving me and carrying away my daughters like captives of the sword?" He is hurt and wounded that the nephew and son-in-law he had trusted and provided for could behave so sneakily. "Why did you flee secretly and deceive me, and did not tell me so that I might have sent you away with joy and with songs, with timbrel and with lyre," Laban's voice grew dramatically mournful. Why did you not allow me to kiss my daughters and grandsons goodbye? Then the anger returned. And why did you take my teraphim?

It is these little idols that Laban is particularly upset about. Why did the teraphim mean so much to him and why did his daughter steal them? It is obvious that Laban still worshipped the gods of old. These teraphim were small idols that served as guardians of his house and family. They may even have symbolized his ancestors. For Laban, they were the heart and soul of his household and without them he feels lost and unprotected. Another reason he may have feared Jacob having them was that possession may have represented a claim to his property.

For Rachel, anxiously leaving her childhood home as she was for the first time in her life, they were a link to her past and her family. Did she think at all of her father's distress at losing them? Or was she too angry at him to care? And if they did indeed represent a claim to the properties, well then, so be it, surely she and Jacob were entitled to it.

Rachel's Clever Ruse

Let not my lord be angry that I cannot rise before you, for the manner of women is upon me.
-Rachel to her Father (Genesis 31:35)

Jacob insisted that he had done Laban no harm, that he had only fled "for I thought that you would take your daughters from me by force." As for the teraphim, he had no idea what Laban was talking about, but gave him permission to search wherever he wanted.

Laban lost no time in a thorough exploration, first in Jacob's tent and then in Leah's. Rachel knew her father would soon be in her tent and discover her secret, one that could destroy them all. Besides, she had no intention of surrendering the teraphim. Did Rachel think up her ploy now, or had she devised her strategy even as she rode away from her father's house? When Laban entered the tent, he found his daughter sitting on the saddle of her camel. Looking up at her father with wide, innocent eyes, Rachel apologized for not getting up, "Let not my lord be angry that I cannot rise before you, for the manner of women is upon me." It was an ingenuous excuse that Laban accepted without question, for what man likes to look closely at matters involving menstruation! And so the idols Rachel had hidden in the saddle remained undiscovered.

Of course Laban does not find what he is seeking and at last Jacob loses patience. "What is my crime?" he protested. "What sin have I committed that you hunt me down? Now that you have searched through all my goods, what have you found that belongs to your household?" For once Laban looked somewhat shamefaced as Jacob enumerated his sins and lack of appreciation. "I have been with you for twenty years now. Your sheep and goats have not miscarried, nor have I eaten rams from your flocks. I did not bring you animals torn by wild beasts; I bore the loss myself."

An Uneasy Truce

Come now, let us make a covenant, you and I,
and let it serve as a witness between us.
-Laban to Jacob (Genesis 31:44)

It is too much for Laban to apologize; even now he seeks to justify his actions with extravagant claims that all is his. "The women are my daughters, the children are my children, and the flocks are my flocks. All you see is mine." But it is a half-hearted assertion and in the end he admits defeat. "Yet what can I do today about these daughters of mine, or about the children they have borne?" Finally he offers to make peace.

They gathered stones and Laban said, "This heap is a witness between you and me today...May the Lord keep watch between you and me when we are away from each other. If you mistreat my daughters or if you take any wives besides my daughters, even though no one is with us, remember that God is a witness between you and me." Then Laban kissed his daughters and grandchildren goodbye, blessed them and left.

Rachel succeeded in keeping the teraphim, but there is a curious epilogue to this chapter. Before Laban had begun his search for the idols, Jacob had uttered words he would never have uttered had he known the truth: "The one with whom you find your gods shall not live." After Laban left, the party continued on their journey and soon after Rachel became pregnant with her second son. She was to die in childbirth. There are those who believe that it was Jacob's unwitting curse that caused his beloved wife to die. But surely God would not have allowed careless words to carry such power. Rachel died simply because death in childbirth was such a common occurrence, and Jacob's words a coincidence.

TAMAR: WIFE, PROSTITUTE, MOTHER

> Your daughter-in-law Tamar is guilty of
> prostitution, and now she's pregnant.
> -Genesis 38:24

When it comes to marital bliss, Tamar, through no fault of her own, is a bust.

Tamar is the wife of Er, who was the son of Judah and grandson of Jacob. When Er dies, Tamar marries her brother-in-law, as was the tradition. When this husband too dies, her father-in-law promises he will give her to his third son. But since this boy is still too young, she must wait. "Live as a widow in your father's house until my son Shelah grows up," he tells her.

Maybe in the beginning Judah had intended to fulfill this promise, but as time passes, he has second thoughts. Is Tamar cursed in some way? If Shelah marries her, "he may die too, just like his brothers." No doubt Shelah also had qualms, wondering if his life would indeed be in danger if he married this woman, his twice-widowed sister-in-law. Then too there was the fact that Tamar was years older than him.

Tamar is frustrated. She is a member of the House of Judah and cannot marry into another family. Yet she comes to realize that her father-in-law has no intention of giving her to his youngest son. She is getting older and at this rate, she will never have a child. So Tamar, not one to sit passively by, takes control of the situation. She will get herself a child, and she intends it to be of the House of Judah.

The plan takes shape. Tamar knows her father-in-law's habits well, one of which is to visit prostitutes. She also knows what roads he uses to get to them, and whether he carries money with him. On this particular day she disguises herself as a harlot, perfumed and veiled, and waits by the side of the road she knows he will take. Sure enough, Judah comes by and when he sees the seductive, beckoning woman, he stops for a bit of diversion.

Because he has no money with him, as Tamar has predicted, she asks for "your seal and its cord and the staff which you hold in your hand," so that she may be paid later. But when Judah sends a friend to make good his pledge, the woman is nowhere to be found. Tamar has left having gotten what she came for and soon she will know that her goal has been achieved.

Three months later, Judah is told that his daughter-in-law is pregnant with some unknown man's child. Judah is incensed at this disgrace to the family. He screams to his men to "bring her out and have her burned to death!"

Tamar appears, and with a sense of high drama, holds up the seal and staff for all to see. "The father of my child is the man to whom these things belong. See if you recognize whose they are."

A stunned Judah realizes that he himself is the father of Tamar's child, and has no right to punish her. Understanding that she did what she did because of his own failure to provide for her, he wisely admits that "she is more in the right than I am, because I did not give her to my son Shelah."

Were Tamar's actions justified? Did she have any other choice? Yes, she could have stayed passively in her father's house growing old and dying and never having a child. But this was not Tamar's way. And God apparently did not penalize her for what she did. He blesses her with a pregnancy and then not one child but twin sons, Peretz and Zerah. As a further indication that God looked kindly upon Tamar, Peretz's descendant is Israel's great hero, King David—which Jesus also claimed as his lineage.

II. FROM JOSEPH'S EGYPT TO MOSES' PROMISED LAND OF CANAAN (1900-1200 BC)

Joseph brings the Jews to Egypt in about 1900 BC where for a time they live in prosperity. But seven centuries later finds them a people enslaved.

Moses will lead them out of Egypt and pass the leadership to Joshua, who will lead them into the land of Canaan. There they will begin to settle down forming the beginnings of cities. No longer nomads, they will begin to build primitive houses and farms.

JOSEPH AND HIS PAGAN WIFE ASENATH PART 1: A MYSTERIOUS HEBREW AND AN INDEPENDENT EGYPTIAN WOMAN

See, I have set you over all the land of Egypt.
-Pharaoh to Joseph (Genesis 41:41)

When Joseph, son of Jacob, marries the daughter of a pagan priest, surprisingly the Lord doesn't seem to mind. In fact, it all seems to be part of the divine plan.

A Daughter of Egypt

What was this wife of one of the heroes of the Book of Genesis like? We know she was the daughter of Potiphera, the priest of On, also known by it's Greek name, Heliopolis, city of the sun. A center of learning, of beautiful temples and architecture, including the impressive obelisks, Heliopolis was devoted to the worship of the sun god Ra. In such an atmosphere, Asenath grows up with reverence and respect for magic and ritual as well as knowledge.

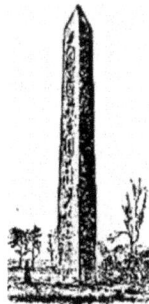

Perhaps this daughter of Egypt is also a devotee of the goddess Seshat whose principal sanctuary was in Heliopolis as well. This goddess was the patron of all forms of writing, of books and of libraries. As a high-born Egyptian woman, Asenath would have had a good education. A tutor would have taught her to read and write hieroglyphics at an early age.

The Bible is stingy with details about Asenath, but rabbinical literature envisions her as a beautiful, intelligent, young maiden who up until meeting the new star of the king's court, is leery of marriage. Her fond father indulges her inclinations until Pharaoh proposes that the daughter of his high priest be given to his trusted minister Joseph.

Now Asenath may be a dutiful daughter and subject, but she will not be bullied into marrying someone she may despise. Still, she has heard the stories about Pharaoh's new minister as who has not, and she is intrigued in spite of herself. The saga of Joseph's spectacular rise from slave to viceroy has been the talk of the royal court. All had been stunned when "Pharaoh took off his signet ring from his hand and put it on Joseph's hand, and clothed him in garments of fine linen and put the gold necklace around his neck."

The king's new favorite is a rather mysterious figure, a foreigner who worships a strange god. How he got to be a slave is a matter for speculation. Some say that Joseph's own brothers sold him into bondage. If that is true, Asenath marvels, he must be especially blessed and protected by his god. After all, how many slaves thrown into prison after being accused of rape by their master's wife would still be alive?

Surely Joseph's master, Potiphar must have suspected the truth from the beginning: his unhappy, unfaithful wife hadn't gotten what she wanted from the good-looking young servant and so had screamed her lie. Her husband pretends to believe her for the sake of his own reputation.

A Revealer of Secrets

Thrown into prison, the innocent victim would have been forgotten but for an extraordinary god-given ability. When two fellow inmates are haunted by disturbing dreams, Joseph is able to reveal their meaning. He correctly predicts that one will live and one will die. They happen to be servants of the king and when the butler is released, he later remembers Joseph's talent when Pharaoh is in need.

It is this magical skill, that of seeing the future through dreams, that so fascinates Asenath. Her father is a powerful priest, but his daughter wonders if he has the powers that Joseph possesses. Certainly none of the sages and magicians that Pharaoh depends on could help him when he was so troubled by nightmares. In desperation, he listens to his butler's recommendation, and to everyone's astonishment, it is this unknown Hebrew who is able to warn the king that his night visions are omens of what lie in store for Egypt. Seven years of plenty followed by seven terrible years of drought. Pharaoh must take action now to forestall disaster by instituting a vast program of grain storage.

The Egyptian sovereign is mightily impressed. Looking deeply into Joseph's honest and intelligent eyes, the king decides that there is no one better to manage this urgent food project than this now ex-slave. Pharaoh bestows the Egyptian name of Zaphenath-paneah or revealer of secrets upon Joseph and makes him the second most powerful man in the land.

PART 2: THE MARRIAGE OF THE JEWISH WISE MAN AND HIS PAGAN BRIDE

A Gift from the Sun

Like Moses after him, Joseph lives the life of a prince of the most sophisticated nation on earth, the center of all learning, far from the rather primitive existence of his childhood. And as Pharaoh becomes ever more fond of his viceroy, he seeks to reward him even further. What better way, than to give him as wife, the lovely daughter of his favorite priest? Doesn't her name, Asenath, mean gift of the sun? She will be my gift to Joseph, Pharaoh decides.

How does Joseph react when his king tells him he is to have the great honor of marrying one of the most sought after women in the land? Is he gratified, excited? Or does he hesitate at the thought of a "mixed marriage?" What would his father say? Yet Joseph is convinced that everything that has happened to him has a purpose, that it is part of God's plan. But what of Asenath; will she come to him willingly?

Joseph does not want a reluctant wife and is prepared to use all of the diplomatic skills he has learned during his years in Egypt to win Asenath. When he was his father's favorite and a rather overbearing child, he had no compunction about lording it over his less loved brothers. Of course he hadn't seen it that way. When he revealed to them his dream that he Joseph would rule over them someday wasn't he just telling his brothers the truth? Now, more mature, he knows that one doesn't always tell the blunt truth in every instance. Joseph's years as a slave have taught him to be patient and cautious, to refrain from hurting others, to wait tactfully for the right moment.

He must tread carefully around his proposed wife. After all, as an Egyptian woman, Asenath would have had more freedom and rights than women of any other country at the time (and more so than many today). She could own property in her own name and should her husband divorce her for any reason other than adultery, he had to give her a substantial portion of his estate. As for education, she would probably have learned to read and write at a far younger age than he Joseph had. Nomadic Hebrews had not yet developed a written language and not until he became an Egyptian slave did he have the opportunity to become literate. Will Asenath consider Joseph beneath her despite his current high status?

He need not worry. Asenath is already strongly attracted to the fascinating, handsome viceroy, and struck by the sincerity in his words and eyes, she readily consents. Did Joseph love Asenath? Romantic love was not an alien concept to the young minister, as he had grown up witnessing one of the greatest love stories in the Bible, that of his father Jacob for his mother Rachel. He had also seen how devastated Jacob was at his mother's early death. But the overwhelming passions of the father are not for the son; Joseph is more sober-minded, more focused on his work, his duties and his god. Moreover, Asenath understands that there is a shadow over his life that keeps Joseph's emotions in check.

He has confided to her his sorrow at the crime his half-brothers committed against him and at the long separation from his father and his full brother Benjamin. Asenath worries that his elderly father may die before he learns the truth about his long lost son. But Joseph is adamant that no message should be sent, for how could he reveal his existence without admitting the evil part that his brothers had played. One day he hopes to introduce her, and hopefully their children, to his father Jacob, but only when God deems it the right time.

To Joseph's relief and happiness, Asenath has no problem conceiving children unlike his mother Rachel, his grandmother Rebekah and his great grandmother Sarah. Yahweh's direct intervention is not needed here, and the young Egyptian wife soon gives birth to a son Manasseh and then a second son Ephraim.

Despite Joseph's occasional melancholy, he and Asenath live a life of contentment and luxury, although not idleness. Under Joseph's able leadership, Egypt continues to store grain for the coming drought and after seven years, just as he predicted, the deadly famine strikes. Egypt alone of all nations is prepared as Joseph carefully sells the grain to the populace.

When they have gone through their money and livestock, Joseph buys their land as well and sets up a system whereby they are given seed to grow on the land they no longer own and give to the government one-fifth of everything they grow.

The Bible claims that the people were happy to do so. "You have saved our lives! Let us find favor in the sight of my lord, and we will be Pharaoh's slaves." Certainly Pharaoh was ecstatic since eventually he owned most of the land in Egypt. But years after the famine had ended; did the people who now owned nothing continue to be satisfied? Could Joseph have found a more equitable solution?

PART 3: IS THAT MY BROTHER? JOSEPH'S FAMILY COMES TO EGYPT

A Momentous Meeting

Famine has assailed the lands far and wide; starvation is rampant. Only Egypt is free from want because of her farseeing viceroy, and outsiders are pouring in. Will Joseph aid those in need? He does, allowing whatever Egypt can spare to be sold. All is going well just as Joseph predicted, yet Asenath knows that beneath his unflappable exterior her husband is in turmoil. Each day he asks himself if this will be the day, the day that he will meet the brothers who sold him into slavery.

That day finally arrives when Joseph receives word that ten men have come from Canaan, men who fit the description that Joseph has given his assistants. He rushes out to see for himself. They do not recognize him; how could they recognize their long-dead brother in this haughty, high-born Egyptian? But Joseph recognizes his ten half brothers. He notes that his full brother Benjamin, the youngest in the family, is not among them.

Jacob's sons are awed to be in the presence of one so great and bow their heads low to the ground. The viceroy speaks in Egyptian and an interpreter translates: who are you, where have you come from?

If the words of the viceroy are foreign, the cold, harsh tone is unmistakable. They tremble, "we are all sons of one man come from the land of Canaan to buy food." But Joseph denies their words, accusing them of treachery. "You are spies; you have come to look at the undefended parts of our land." What game is Joseph playing, and why is he pretending ignorance of their language?

"No, my lord," the brothers insist, "but your servants have come to buy food." The viceroy pins them with his piercing eyes and demands details of their lives. Who is your father, do you have other brothers? Jacob is our father they tell him. "Your servants are twelve brothers in all, the sons of one man in the land of Canaan; and behold, the youngest is with our father today, and one is no longer alive."

"We are honest men; your servants are not spies." But Joseph is implacable. "It is as I said to you, you are spies; by this you will be tested: by the life of Pharaoh, you shall not go from this place unless your youngest brother comes here!" Then we will see if there is truth in you.

Refusing to listen to anymore protestations, the viceroy sweeps out. To the brothers' dismay, guards seize them and drag them to a prison cell. There they remain for three days until the viceroy sends for them.

This is just a taste of what will befall you if you are lying, he threatens. But "if you are honest men, let one of your brothers be confined here in prison; as for the rest of you, go, carry grain for your households, and bring your youngest brother to me, so your words may be verified, and you will not die."

The brothers talk among themselves not realizing that the viceroy understands every word they speak. In their minds the picture of their young brother Joseph's sufferings long ago at their hands is strong. "Truly we are guilty concerning our brother, because we saw the distress of his soul when he pleaded with us, yet we would not listen; therefore this distress has come upon us." Reuben, the oldest looks grim, "did I not tell you, 'Do not sin against the boy'; and you would not listen? Now comes the reckoning for his blood."

At their speech, the viceroy is overcome. He flees the room so that no one may see him weep. These words of confession of guilt are what he has been waiting for, he tells Asenath when she sees her stoic husband's emotion-charged face. Surely, then, it is time to reveal the truth to his brothers. But Joseph says the testing is not yet done.

Jacob's Quandary

The viceroy leaves orders that the brothers may fill their sacks with grain. All may leave; all that is except one. Simeon, the second son is to remain as prisoner until the bargain is fulfilled and the youngest son, Benjamin, brought to Egypt.

With full sacks upon their shoulders and minds rife with fear, the brothers begin their trek home. Along the way, they discover to their astonishment that the money they used to pay for the grain is back in their sacks, a circumstance which only adds to their anxious bewilderment. How will they explain all to their father, most particularly that one son is in prison and another must return with them?

Did Joseph spare a thought as to how his aged father would react to events? Or was he too obsessed with his grand plan? Jacob is devastated and angry as well, which he takes out on his sons. "You have bereaved me of my children: Joseph is no more, and Simeon is no more, and you would take Benjamin; all these things are against me."

A desperate Reuben tries to convince his father to allow Benjamin to return with them to Egypt. "You may put my two sons to death if I do not bring him back to you; put him in my care, and I will return him to you."

But Jacob is adamant. "My son shall not go down with you; for his brother is dead, and he alone is left. If harm should befall him on the journey you are taking, then you will bring my gray hair down to Sheol in sorrow."

Not even Jacob, however, can battle the continuing famine, and there comes a time when the food brought back from Egypt is nearly gone. You must go back he tells his sons. Judah reminds him of the viceroy's warning, "You shall not see my face unless your brother is with you." He beseeches his father to "send the lad with me and we will arise and go, that we may live and not die, we as well as you and our little ones."

At last Jacob relents knowing he has little choice. The brothers are soon on their way along with the gifts that Jacob has urged upon them to soften the Egyptians: "a little balm and a little honey, aromatic gum and myrrh, pistachio nuts and almonds." And "Take double the money in your hand, and take back in your hand the money that was returned in the mouth of your sacks; perhaps it was a mistake." Jacob sinks to the ground as his sons disappear from sight, shuddering at what fresh losses await him; and the nature of the powerful man who holds his family's life in his hands.

Return to the Lion's Den

Once they enter Egypt, the brothers are prepared for anything. Yet once again, the viceroy leaves them gaping. Instead of the cruel treatment they expect, the steward brings them to Joseph's house for dinner where Simeon is restored to them. Joseph enters looking much kindlier than before. The brothers bow low and present him with their gifts.

"Then he asked them about their welfare, and said, 'is your old father well, of whom you spoke? Is he still alive?'"

Yes, "your servant our father is well; he is still alive."

Joseph pointed to Benjamin. "Is this your youngest brother, of whom you spoke to me?" And he spoke directly to Benjamin, "may God be gracious to you, my son." As Benjamin looked him full in the face, "he was deeply stirred over his brother, and he sought a place to weep."

The viceroy excuses himself, once again emotion overwhelming him, for this was his full brother, the son of his mother Rachel. Benjamin had never

known their mother as she had died giving birth to him. But before Joseph
had been sold as a slave, he had regaled his little brother with his memories
of Rachel. Now as he remembers those times, tears run freely. Only his wife
is there to see. She handed him a cloth, and "then he washed his face and
he controlled himself."

The meal is served when Joseph reenters the room. The brothers can
hardly accept what is happening. "They were seated before him, the
firstborn according to his birthright and the youngest according to his
youth, and the men looked at one another in astonishment." Even more
amazing is the viceroy taking "portions to them from his own table." As
usual in this family, favorites are played, and "Benjamin's portion was five
times as much as any of theirs."

The brothers begin to relax and "feasted and drank freely with him."
Then privately the viceroy ordered his steward to "fill the men's sacks with
food, as much as they can carry, and put each man's money in the mouth of
his sack. And put my cup, the silver cup, in the mouth of the sack of the
youngest, and his money for the grain."

With the coming of dawn, the brothers set off with their sacks and their
donkeys. But no sooner had they left the city when they were overtaken by
the viceroy's men. The steward accuses them of theft. They protest their
innocence, but the cup is discovered in Benjamin's sack.

"Then they tore their clothes, and when each man loaded his donkey,
they returned to the city. When Judah and his brothers came to Joseph's
house, they fell to the ground before him," offering themselves as his
slaves. But Joseph declares that only the guilty one shall be his slave, while
the rest may go in peace.

"Then Judah approached him, and said, 'Oh my lord, may your servant
please speak a word in my lord's ears, and do not be angry with your
servant; for you are equal to Pharaoh." He begged the viceroy to
reconsider. If they did not return with Benjamin, their father would die.

Revelation

At these words, Joseph could not control himself," and dismissed all the Egyptians until he was alone with his brothers. There are no more plans and plots in the viceroy's head. Look at me; he tells them, "I am your brother Joseph, whom you sold into Egypt." And "he wept so loudly that the Egyptians heard it, and the household of Pharaoh heard of it."

The brothers stare; the viceroy's words make no sense. Joseph steps closer. "Behold, your eyes see, and the eyes of my brother Benjamin see, that it is my mouth which is speaking to you." Slowly, understanding seeps in. And at last they believe and tears begin to course down their faces.

"Then he fell on his brother Benjamin's neck and wept, and Benjamin wept on his neck. He kissed all his brothers and wept on them, and afterward his brothers talked with him."

"Now do not be grieved or angry with yourselves, because you sold me here," Joseph declares that God had a purpose in sending him into Egypt, that he was sent to save lives. God "made me a father to Pharaoh and lord of all his household and ruler over all the land of Egypt."

The famine will rage for five more years, Joseph tells his brothers, but there is no need to worry "You shall live in the land of Goshen, and you shall be near me, you and your children and your children's children. I will give you the best of the land of Egypt and you will eat the fat of the land."

Now they must return home and "tell my father of all my splendor in Egypt, and all that you have seen; and you must hurry and bring my father down here."

Jacob and his Sons Settle in Egypt

When Jacob is first told that his beloved son still lives, "and indeed is ruler over all the land of Egypt," he is angered, believing this to be a cruel and fantastical tale. But when he looked at all the wagons loaded with provisions, and his sons repeated all that Joseph had told them, Jacob rose up with renewed hope. He is still wary of believing fully in the reality of Joseph's survival; that will not come until he and his son are face to face. But with a sudden strength he has not known for many years, Jacob is eager to be on his way.

"Joseph prepared his chariot and went up to Goshen to meet his father; as soon as he appeared before him, he fell on his neck and wept a long time." Jacob proclaims that he would be happy to die now, "since I have seen your face, that you are still alive."

Asenath is elated at the family reunion, yet worries that Jacob may reject her and her children. Jacob, however, shares his son's belief that Asenath too was part of God's plan. He is delighted with his two grandsons and lest there be any doubt that they are truly part of the tribe, Jacob declares in a kind of adoption that "Now your two sons, who were born to you in the land of Egypt before I came to you in Egypt, are mine; Ephraim and Manasseh shall be mine, as Reuben and Simeon are."

Yet if Jacob acknowledged his daughter-in-law and her children, the teachers of later centuries had a more difficult time of it. So disturbed were they at a pagan woman's marriage to a saintly Israelite, that stories were concocted changing Asenath's Egyptian polytheistic heritage. In one particularly bizarre tale, Asenath is made to be the illegitimate child of Joseph's half-sister Dinah and the man who raped her! Thus Joseph marries his own niece, conceived in violence, which was felt to be preferable than marrying a pagan Egyptian. In another less convoluted saga, Asenath simply abandons the worship of her own Egyptian gods in favor of Jehovah.

But the fact remains that nowhere in the Bible is there any mention of conversion. Despite that, the unconverted Asenath and her Israelite husband live out their lives in peace and harmony, beautiful, glamorous, successful, the power couple of their day.

A RIBBON OF RED AND THE FALL OF JERICHO: RAHAB THE HARLOT

The children of Israel might never have made it to the Promised Land were it not for the help of a harlot. The question is: was Rahab a heroine or a traitor?

Rahab is living in Canaan in its major city Jericho, one of the loveliest and oldest cities in the world, plying her trade, when the Hebrews emerge from their long years in the wilderness and begin the final leg of their journey. Her house is strategically located just inside the city wall of Jericho, allowing her to attract customers as people go in and out of the gated town. Rahab knows just about everything about everybody and is the first person even the King of Jericho goes to when he needs information.

Why Rahab became a prostitute the Bible doesn't tell us. It certainly isn't because she is alone in the world and without family. In fact she has a mother and father, sisters, and brothers. Did her father force her into a cruel marriage perhaps, a union that Rahab could not tolerate and ran away from? We simply don't know. But Rahab is no downtrodden hooker. She is an independent and strong willed woman.

Now, however, like the town's other inhabitants, she is frightened. News has spread that a strange group of people, once slaves in Egypt, are on their way to conquer her city because their god has told them to. Fantastic tales of how this god parted the sea, and how the Israelites destroyed Sihon and Og, the two kings of the Amorites east of the Jordan, is spreading panic throughout the population.

Rahab Strikes a Deal with the Enemy

The Canaanites have good reason to be afraid, for the Israelites—camped nearby—are plotting their attack against the city next on their list. Joshua has become their leader following the death of Moses. He is an accomplished soldier and savvy strategist. Now he sends two spies to report on the powerful and heavily protected city. The two young men eventually wind up at the house of Rahab. Do they go there for the obvious reason? Are they looking for a place to stay and does Rahab rent out her rooms? Or do they know that Rahab is a good source of information and her house a good place from which to analyze the city's defenses?

Whatever the reason, these two primitive desert wanderers must have been amazed at the sight of this sophisticated city woman with her bracelets and rings, reddened lips, and seductive clothing. She invites them in and immediately guesses their identities. Slowly a plan begins to percolate in her mind. I know who you are she tells the Hebrew spies and I will help you.

Now the king of Jericho has his own grapevine and has gotten wind that some suspicious characters have entered Rahab's house. The king sends his guards who order her to "bring out the men who came to you and entered your house, because they have come to spy out the whole land." Rahab opens her door smiling and lets the king's guards in to look around. "Yes, the men came to me, but I did not know where they had come from. At dusk, when it was time to close the city gate, the men left. I don't know which way they went. Go after them quickly. You may catch up with them."

As soon as the disappointed guards rush out in pursuit, Rahab runs up to the roof. There, hiding beneath abundant stalks of flax, are the two Israelite spies, just where Rahab has left them. Rahab has thrown in her lot with the enemy. Why is she so ready to betray the city she lives in? Have Jericho's rulers angered her? Treated her badly? Or is she convinced that the god of the Hebrews is invincible and that their victory inevitable? Indeed she tells the two young men that "your God is God in heaven above and on the earth below," and that "the Lord has given this land to you."

So why not take advantage of this opportunity to be on the winning side? Perhaps it is the Hebrew god himself who is offering her this chance. Rahab has not survived this long by sitting passively by. She has saved the life of the two spies, and now she asks for her payback. "Please swear to me by the Lord that you will show kindness to my family, because I have shown kindness to you. Give me a sure sign that you will spare the lives of my father and mother, my brothers and sisters, and all who belong to them, and that you will save us from death."

The two spies know that but for Rahab, they would have faced torture and death. Gratefully, the Israelites swear an oath that as long as Rahab doesn't betray them after they leave, she will be safe. "Our lives for your lives!" the men assure her. "If you don't tell what we are doing, we will treat you kindly and faithfully when the Lord gives us the land." They leave her with strict instructions that her family must be inside her house in order to be spared and that she should hang a red ribbon in the window so that the Israelite army will recognize her house.

The deal is done. There is no turning back now for Rahab. She lets the two down by a rope, and they take her advice to hide themselves in the hills until the hunt for them is over. For three days the king's men search up and down the roads finally giving up and returning to the city and their king empty-handed. The spies are now free to return to their camp, mission accomplished. Joshua welcomes them back and is satisfied to hear Rahab's words that "all who live in this country are melting in fear because of you."

A City is Devoted to the Lord

The time has come for Rahab to prepare for the fall of Jericho. First she must persuade her estranged family to stay at her house; not an easy task. Rahab, after all, is an embarrassment to them, and perhaps there is also much she doesn't like in her parents and siblings as well. Still, she cares for them and passionately wants to save their lives. But here is a terrible problem. She may save her immediate family but what about uncles, aunts, cousins? What about friends? She cannot save all these people and so she must choose a precious few among them and essentially condemn the rest.

Somehow she succeeds in getting her relatives safely into her house. The last thing she must do is put up the red ribbon. Rahab doesn't know it, but the ribbon of red is reminiscent of the lamb's blood that the Hebrews smeared on their doors so that God would "pass over" their house and kill only Egypt's firstborn.

On the fateful day, Joshua and his men begin their campaign. Obeying the Lord's instructions, they march around the city for six days. With them are the priests carrying the ark. On the seventh day they march around seven times, Joshua shouts that "the Lord has given you the city," and the walls simply crumble! But it is not likely that the people of Jericho would have gone like lambs to the slaughter. Even after being demoralized by the ruin of their protective wall, they would have fought. The men would have been organized into an armed force and there would have been a battle with Israelites dying as well as their enemies. Even the women would have fought.

Eventually, however, Joshua's army overcomes whatever armed resistance there is, and "they devote the city to the Lord." That is, they destroy by sword "every living thing in it-men and women, young and old, cattle, sheep and donkeys." If there were any people left in the houses such as the sick, elderly or infants, they would have died when the soldiers "burned the whole city and everything in it, but put the silver and gold and the articles of bronze and iron into the treasury of the Lord's house." Only Rahab and her people are spared in fulfillment of the agreement.

When it is over, where once there was a thriving town, there is now only rubble and charred remains. Militarily, Joshua has won a tremendous victory. All of the other Canaanite cities know they had better surrender or else. But why did God demand such an act of total destruction? Certainly we are not told that Jericho was a wicked city like Sodom and Gomorrah. We know only that in the Book of Joshua, God is a god of war who seems to revel in battles and victories over enemy armies; a god who deems those who do not worship him as being unworthy of life.

For this reason, the very ground on which Jericho stood is considered evil. No man, not even the Israelites, may build here. "Cursed before the Lord is the man who undertakes to rebuild this city, Jericho," Joshua intones. "At the cost of his firstborn son will he lay its foundations; at the cost of his youngest will he set up its gates."

The Devastation: Did Rahab Realize?

Did Rabab realize how complete the devastation would be? Would she have made the same decision had she known that the people of Jericho were to become a mass sacrifice to an alien god? Is Rahab a heroine, or a traitor? To the Israelites she is a great heroine who helped contribute to their victory. She and her family are given honored places among the Israelites. For the people of Jericho (if any had survived), a different answer might have been given.

A number of traditions have grown up around Rahab. In each of these, Rahab gives up the oldest profession, accepts the faith of the Hebrews and earns a place of respect among the Israelites. In the book of Matthew in the New Testament, she is mentioned as the mother of Boaz, who is the ancestor of King David and Jesus. According to the Talmud, she marries Joshua and can count a number of prophets as her descendents. Last but not least other Talmudic accounts refer to Rahab as one of the most beautiful women in the world, so beautiful in fact that just saying her name could engender desire.

To herself, Rahab may have been neither heroine nor traitor, but simply a survivor who makes tough choices in the face of impossible conditions. Through her initiative and spunk, she manages to save herself and her family. Does she ever think about the city that died? Does she remember the people she once knew, who perished on that terrible day? The Bible simply doesn't tell us. We are left with silence, and an overwhelming sense of having witnessed the life of a powerful woman.

HOLY AND LETHAL: THE ARK OF THE COVENANT
PART 1: A BOX WITH TWO STONES (AND A SEAT FOR GOD)

> There, above the cover between the two
> cherubim, I will meet with you and give you all
> my commands.
> -God to Moses (Exodus 25:22)

There is no more sacred object in the Bible than the Ark of the Covenant. But what exactly is the Ark? And what was its power that its mere presence could cause misery and suffering, while touching it could cause death?

The ark first makes its appearance when the Lord instructs Moses to create a box for the soon to come Ten Commandments. God is very specific on how this should be built. It must be of acacia wood, measuring a little less than four feet long and a little over two feet wide and high. God tells Moses to use lots of gold: "Overlay it with pure gold, both inside and out, and make a gold molding around it." Two wooden poles also inlaid with gold will be inserted in the gold rings that will carry it.

However the ark is not only a container for the laws, but a multi-purpose device. On the top rests a solid block of pure gold, known as the atonement cover. It is upon this block that God will sit between two gold cherubim when he meets with Moses. Here too is where the Lord stays when he accompanies the Israelites on their way to the Promised Land.

When the Israelites make camp, the ark resides in "the Holy of Holies, the innermost room of the Tabernacle" or Tent of Meeting, a portable sanctuary whose frame and curtains can be dismantled and rolled up when the group is on the move.

From the beginning the ark is a complex symbol of both reassurance and danger. It leads an uncertain people on their journey: "When you see the ark of the covenant of the Lord your God, and the priests, who are Levites, carrying it, you are to move out from your positions and follow it. Then you will know which way to go, since you have never been this way before." Yet the Israelites are also constantly warned to beware, to "keep a distance of about a thousand yards between you and the ark; do not go near it."

They soon learn just how lethal the ark can be when the two priest sons of Aaron, Nadab and Abihu, are struck dead in the Tabernacle for "offering unauthorized fire before the Lord, contrary to his command." The brothers, with the best of intentions, had burned incense in their pans to honor the Lord in the sanctuary. But God had not specifically designated them to do that at that particular time. "So fire came out from the presence of the Lord and consumed them."

The people are horrified at the deaths of these two young men, and Yahweh rather testily orders Moses to "tell your brother Aaron not to come whenever he chooses into the Most Holy Place behind the curtain in front of the atonement cover on the ark, or else he will die, because I appear in the cloud over the atonement cover." Thereafter careful preparations are made in terms of time, appropriate dress, anointing with oil, and proper sacrifices.

But when a miracle is needed, the ark can provide one. When the Israelites come to the Jordan River—the entrance way to the Promised Land—they despair of ever getting across. But just as the Red Sea parted, so do the waters of the River Jordan recede before the power of the ark. "The priests who carried the ark of the covenant of the Lord stood firm on dry ground in the middle of the Jordan, while all Israel passed by until the whole nation had completed the crossing." Then the priests followed, and "the waters of the Jordan returned to their place and ran at flood stage as before."

Once in the Promised Land, the ark plays a key role in helping defeat the inhabitants who live there. Before the battle of Jericho, the ark is marched around the city for seven days and as a result, the Bible tells us, the walls disintegrate. This permits the Israelites to march in and destroy the town according to God's plan.

PART 2: DISASTER, THE ARK IS CAPTURED

> After the Philistines had captured the ark of
> God, they took it from Ebenezer to Ashdod.
> -1 Samuel 5:1

With the Israelites now established in the land of Canaan, the ark settles down in the temple at Shiloh. It is nearby, during the time of the Judges, that the Israelites are soundly defeated by their perpetual enemies, the Philistines. Morale is sinking steadily when the Israelite commanders are inspired to bring down the ark to shore up the army's confidence. At first the idea seems a good one, for as the ark appears the troops "raise such a great shout that the ground shakes." The enemy too is mightily impressed and fearful. "A god has come into the camp," the word spreads. "Woe to us! Who will deliver us from the hand of these mighty gods?!"

But instead of backing down, the clever Philistine general uses the ark's presence to motivate his men to fight even harder: "Be strong, Philistines! Be men, or you will be subject to the Hebrews, as they have been to you. Be men, and fight!" The Philistines do just that, dealing their opponent a calamitous defeat. Not only are thirty thousand foot soldiers lost, but the ark is captured!

The town of Shiloh with its many men in the Israelite army waits fearfully for news. One woman in particular is nervously pacing the floor of her house, although she is over eight months pregnant. She is the wife of Phinehas, son of Eli the priest, who accompanied the ark along with his brother Hophni. To add to her worries, her father-in-law Eli insists on sitting by the roadside even though at 98 he is extremely frail. But he must hear the news as soon as possible he tells her. His sons are in danger and as for the ark itself—it was in his care. Should anything befall his precious charge, he must answer to God.

Suddenly Eli hears screams and cries. "What is the meaning of the uproar," he trembles and the messenger hurries over to him. The man is exhausted, with his clothes torn and dust on his head, but with all that has happened today, he still shudders at the thought of what he must tell the old man. There is nothing for it but to say it outright: "Israel fled before the Philistines, and the army has suffered heavy losses. Also your two sons, Hophni and Phinehas, are dead, and the ark of God has been captured."

Before the messenger can catch him, Eli falls backward in shock and when the messenger quickly bends over him, he realizes that Eli is dead, his neck broken. The unfortunate family is doomed to suffer still more tragedy for when Eli's daughter-in-law hears that her husband and father-in-law are both dead, she goes into labor. As her son is born, she whispers his name Ichabod. It is a sad name that means "the glory has departed" for with the ark gone Israel is bereft. Then she too dies leaving her newborn child an orphan.

Divine Vengeance: Hemorrhoids and Mice

> And he smote the men of the city, both small
> and great, and they had hemorrhoids in their
> secret parts.
> -1 Samuel 5:9

With a great victory and the magical ark in their hands, the Philistines are in high spirits. They are well aware of what value their enemy places on this sacred object and its alleged connections with the Hebrew god. Surely its power will flow favorably to whoever possesses it like a good luck charm.

In their own way, the Philistines respect the ark and when their general arrives in the city of Ashdod, he sets it in a place of honor in the temple next to a statue of his own god Dagon. Thus the ark is seen as an equal to their own revered deity. Of course, Yahweh doesn't see it that way and upon entering the temple the next morning, the priest is startled to discover the statue of Dagon "prostrate before it (the ark)." The priest restores the statue, but the next day is aghast to find Dagon once again flat on the ground before the ark, and this time with his head and hands broken off as well!

The shattered idol is just the beginning of the troubles of the city. With a punishing sense of humor, God strikes the people of Ashdod with an epidemic of hemorrhoids. And to further torment them, the Lord sends a plague of mice.

Sensing the connection between the presence of the ark and their miseries, it isn't long before the people of Ashdod are screaming to the authorities to get rid of that golden box. "So they called together all the rulers of the Philistines, "What shall we do with the ark of the god of Israel," they demand to know. Still determined to keep possession despite the havoc that the sacred box is causing, the leaders decide that a change of scenery might solve the problem, so they "have the ark of the god of Israel moved to Gath."

The people of Ashdod breathe a sigh of relief as the ark rolls out of town. Yet the hopes of the Philistines are soon dashed when in no time the people of Gath are also attacked by hemorrhoids and rodents. Panic-stricken, the populace evicts the golden box, sending it to the city of Ekron. But news of the ark's vengeful powers has spread, and before it can enter the city, the townspeople try to bar the way, crying that "they have brought the ark of the god of Israel around to us to kill us and our people." And they beg their king to "send the ark of the god of Israel away; let it go back to its own place."

Guilt Offerings of Gold

After seven months and five afflicted cities, the Philistines are at a loss. What was supposed to be a grand triumph has turned into a dreadful farce. They long to rid themselves of this troublesome box, but how? So the Philistine rulers summon the priests and the diviners. "What shall we do with the ark of the Lord? Tell us how we should send it back to its place."

The Philistine priests ponder the problem and being a wise and practical lot, perceive that it won't be enough to simply send it back. The ark must be returned with an acknowledgement of wrongdoing, a "guilt offering," and one that, properly, must reflect the plagues that the Israelite god has struck them with. You must make models of a hemorrhoid and a mouse, instruct the priests. There must be five of each for the five cities and they must be made of gold. In that way, you will "pay honor to Israel's god."

When the gold hemorrhoids and mice are ready, they are placed inside a cart alongside the ark. With two cows hitched to the cart, it is sent on its way as the Philistines fervently pray that this is the end of their woes.

PART 3: JOY (AND HORROR): THE RETURN OF THE ARK

> Then David was angry because the Lord's wrath
> had broken out against Uzzah
> -2 Samuel 6:8

With God leading them, the animals head straight for the Israelite town of Beth Shemesh where the people are in the fields busy harvesting their wheat. Suddenly a great shout is heard and "when they looked up and saw the ark, they rejoiced at the sight." A crowd gathers around the object so central to their faith, inspiring them with renewed hope for the future.

Unfortunately, their optimism soon turns bitter because of a very human trait: curiosity. Here is an opportunity, think some of the men, to closely examine the awe inspiring object. But although curiosity may be a very human emotion, it is one that God did not always tolerate, as witness Eve and the punishment accorded her desire for knowledge. The Lord had very strict rules about his ark, and should one break those rules, no matter how innocent seeming the act, God wouldn't hesitate to kill. Thus, "God strikes down the men of Beth Shemesh, putting seventy of them to death because they had looked into the ark of the Lord."

"The people mourned because of the heavy blow the Lord had dealt them." And they wonder, "Who can stand in the presence of the Lord, this holy God? To whom will the ark go up from here?"

There is fear now and grave doubt that anyone in the land can care for this object of terror. The Israelite leaders confer and finally an answer is found. The ark is sent to Kiriath Jearim, where it is taken to Abinadab's house on the hill and peacefully guarded by him and his son Eleazar for many years.

A Rough Road: the Ark Heads for Jerusalem

Time passes and David is made king of all Israel. To commemorate the event, the king is planning the grandest celebration that Israel has ever seen. The highlight of the show will be the entry of the Ark of the Covenant into the new political and religious capital of Jerusalem.

Taking an impressive escort of 30,000, David goes to the house of Abinadab to oversee the moving of this precious piece. Carefully it is placed in a cart, guided by Abinadab's sons, Uzzah and Ahio. Everything is going smoothly and the king is ecstatic as "the whole house of Israel celebrates with all their might before the Lord, with songs and with harps, lyres, tambourines, sistrums and cymbals."

Alas, as so often happens, the ark proves to be a mixed blessing. A rough spot in the road causes the oxen to stumble and the cart to wobble, threatening to overturn and damage the ark. Uzzah, an upright and responsible man who thinks only to protect the ark, reaches out his hand to steady it. But Uzzah's good intentions are irrelevant next to God's implacable rule that the ark not be touched.

"The Lord's anger burned against Uzzah because of his irreverent act; therefore God struck him down and he died there beside the ark of God."

Suddenly the party becomes a wake. And the king, so happy a moment before, is plunged into fear and dismay. He doubts whether God wants him to take the ark into Jerusalem, the city of David. "How can the ark of the Lord ever come to me?"

Frustrated, the king sends the ark to the house of a pious individual, Obed-Edom the Gittite for safekeeping. Here the box will stay until David is absolutely certain that the Lord does indeed want him to take it. Three months pass and the king is told that the Lord has blessed Obed-Edom and his entire household. Exactly what form the blessing took, we aren't told, but David takes that to mean that God approves of his plans.

"So David went down and brought up the ark of God from the house of Obed-Edom to the City of David with rejoicing. When those who were carrying the ark of the Lord had taken six steps, he sacrificed a bull and a fattened calf." Then the king does a passionate dance of triumph, as "the entire house of Israel brought up the ark of the Lord with shouts and the sound of trumpets."

The Temple: A Magnificent New Abode for the Ark

Although David establishes the ark in Jerusalem, the Lord tells him that "you are not the one to build the temple, but your son, who is your own flesh and blood—he is the one who will build the temple for my Name." It is Solomon who spares no expense in building the ark's new home, the center of religious worship in Israel. "On the walls all around the temple, in both the inner and outer rooms, he carved cherubim, palm trees and open flowers. He also covered the floors of both the inner and outer rooms of the temple with gold."

At last the temple is complete and "King Solomon and the entire assembly of Israel that had gathered about him were before the ark, sacrificing so many sheep and cattle that they could not be recorded or counted."

God was obviously pleased because "when the priests withdrew from the Holy Place, the cloud filled the temple of the Lord." So immense was God's presence in fact that "the priests could not perform their service because of the cloud, for the glory of the Lord filled his temple." Delighted, the king—somewhat immodestly—addresses God, "I have indeed built a magnificent temple for you, a place for you to dwell forever."

Yet even in this supreme moment of Solomon's reign lie the beginnings of Israel's downfall. For Solomon was a most extravagant monarch, provoking discontent among his subjects with his excessive taxes and numerous building projects for his own glory. When he dies, the nation splits apart, never to be united again. And with its dissolution the Ark of the Covenant is spoken of no more, its fate a mystery.

PART 4: THE BEST OF THE ARK (THE UNKNOWN SECOND TEN COMMANDMENTS)

With its history of affliction, one might think the ark solely a symbol of misery. Yet it also represents words of wisdom. God gave Moses not only the Ten Commandments, but many other principles with which to live by. Some of these rules are clearly meant for a people living long ago. "Do not offer the blood of a sacrifice to me along with anything containing yeast," was obviously meant for those still practicing animal sacrifice.

Yet other precepts are incredibly enlightened, and even sophisticated, if not always easy to live up to.*

Do not go along with the crowd in doing wrong.

Never give false testimony on a witness stand because of pressure from evil people or the majority.

Do not discriminate against someone in a lawsuit because they are poor, nor show favoritism towards them for the same reason.

Never get involved in false accusations or put an innocent person to death for "I will not allow anyone guilty of this to go free."

Never accept a bribe, for a bribe will blind you to the truth and cause you to ignore and hurt the person who is in the right.

Do not oppress foreigners; you yourselves know how it feels to be foreigners, because you were foreigners in Egypt.

Although the golden box was lost, the best of what it symbolized is still with us.

*These precepts are from Exodus 23:2-9

III. JUDGES: THE JEWISH TRIBAL CHIEFTAINS
(1200-1000 BC)

When the Jewish tribes first settle down in Canaan after the exodus, they are loosely ruled by judges, who are really tribal chieftains. It is a dark age of perhaps two centuries full of violence and brutality. Instead of the unity they knew under Moses and Joshua, the Israelites regress into a primitive tribalism where they fight each other as often as they fight "outsiders."

Not until Saul becomes Israel's first king, do the tribes unite into one nation.

DEADLY FEMALE DUO: JUDGE DEBORAH AND EXECUTIONER JAEL

When the Canaanite King Jabin conquers the Israelites, little does he know that he will be defeated by a deadly feminine duo, the Jewish Deborah and the non-Jewish Kenite woman, Jael.

Deborah is ancient Israel's only female judge. How she got to be a judge in about 1100 BC, the Bible doesn't say, but we can assume that she had to be pretty tough to attain such a position in a society where women were little better than property. She is also a prophetess and later a military leader, a rare combination for the male prophets much less a female one. And since this was the period before the establishment of the monarchy, where judges and prophets were the leaders and the law, Deborah was especially powerful.

Of her personal life, we know little except that she was married to a man named Lappidoth. We learn about Deborah only through the work she does. The judge holds court at "the palm tree of Deborah," and if the Israelite men are at first reluctant to bring their disputes to a woman, her clear, just pronouncements win their respect.

God Sends a Message to Deborah

During this time, Israel is suffering under the yoke of King Jabin the Canaanite and his general Sisera. They have overwhelmed the Israelites with their superior military technology. "Because he had nine hundred iron chariots and has cruelly oppressed the Israelites for twenty years, they cried to the Lord for help." God hears their entreaties and charges Deborah with freeing his people.

As a prophet, Deborah would have heard the Lord through dreams and visions. Awake she feels the heavy responsibility of mobilizing the populace to do more than just complain. At last Deborah sends for the Israelite commander Barak and directs him to gather an army of ten thousand men and "lead the way to Mount Tabor. I will lure Sisera, the commander of Jabin's army, with his chariots and his troops to the Kishon River and give him into your hands."

Barak is hesitant and agrees only with conditions, "If you go with me, I will go; but if you don't go with me, I won't go." Barak certainly doesn't seem like a very strong leader and Deborah somewhat tauntingly returns "Very well, I will go with you. But because of the way you are going about this, the honor will not be yours, for the Lord will hand Sisera over to a woman." Despite this, Barak accepts the terms, his confidence in Deborah and the need to defeat the Canaanites overcoming his reluctance.

So Deborah and Barak go off to ready an army. Not all Israelites are enthusiastic about battling the Canaanites. Many doubt that God has truly spoken to her and lack confidence in Barak. We cannot win they think. Better to remain beneath the heel of the Canaanites then to be murdered by them in their chariots. Later Deborah will denounce those who refused to fight such as the tribes of Dan who "stayed in ships," Asher who "sat at the seashore," and Gilead who "remained across the Jordan." But there are others who willingly take up arms against their oppressors and are later praised by the prophet: "the princes of Issachar were with Deborah," and Ephraim, Benjamin, Manasseh, Zebulun, and Naphtali all "fought the kings of Canaan."

A Battle and the Stars in Heaven

When ten thousand men are assembled, Deborah and Barak formulate their battle plans. Finally they are ready and on that day Deborah proclaims before all that God is on their side "Go! This is the day the Lord has given Sisera into your hands. Has not the Lord gone ahead of you?" Barak and his men go down Mount Tabor sure that heaven is with them. But a fearsome sight meets their eyes.

The Canaanite army, in all their glory with their magnificent chariots, is waiting for them in the plain of Megiddo. At their head is Sisera, a man well versed in the arts of war.

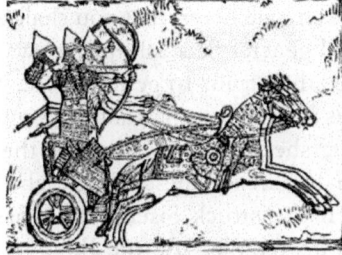

Yet just as Deborah has told them, the Lord is with the Israelite forces and as the "stars fight from heaven," the Israelites "rout Sisera and all his chariots and army by the sword." The triumphant Barak and his men pursue whatever soldiers remain until "all the troops of Sisera fell by the sword; not a man was left." Except for one--with his army wiped out, Sisera abandons his chariot and escapes on foot.

Desperately the beaten general runs to the home of an ally of his and the king's: Heber the Kenite "for there was peace between Jabin the king of Hazor and the house of Heber the Kenite." This Heber has separated himself from his fellow tribesmen who are friends of the Israelites and instead joined himself to the Canaanites. He has pitched his tent far away from the other Kenites. It is here that Sisera knows he will be safe.

A Peg, a Hammer, and Death

But Heber is not at home, only his wife. Jael has heard the battle cries and has been watching from her tent when she sees a figure she recognizes in the distance. What Sisera does not know is that Jael violently disagrees with her husband's choice of allies. But she has kept silent in front of Heber as he boasts of generous rewards to come from the Canaanites.

Jael goes out to meet Sisera and with sympathy in her eyes says to him, "Turn aside, my master, turn aside to me! Do not be afraid." Gratefully the general follows Jael as she welcomes him into her home. Slowly a plan begins to form in Jael's head. Can she do it she wonders or will she herself wind up dead? Sisera may be worn out but he is nevertheless big and strong and a fighting man. Still, perhaps God himself is giving her this opportunity.

Jael does everything to make Sisera comfortable even covering him with a rug. When he asks for water, Jael gives him a soothing drink of milk instead. Gradually the weary general begins to relax in the presence of this motherly woman despite the horrible defeat he has suffered. He will gather another army, he thinks optimistically, and this time he will destroy the Israelites. His eyes begin to grow heavy and he turns to his hostess "Stand in the doorway of the tent, and it shall be if anyone comes and inquires of you, and says, 'Is there anyone here?' that you shall say, 'No.'"

Soon the exhausted general falls asleep. Jael waits and watches. Sisera's mind and body calmed, he begins to gently snore. Now is the moment she tells herself while he is heavily asleep. Taking a tent peg in one hand, and a hammer in the other, she slowly approaches the quiet figure, watching carefully for any sign of wakefulness. Softly she places the peg against Sisera's temple. "Then she struck Sisera, she smashed his head, and she shattered and pierced his temple." As the Bible so graphically describes it, the peg goes right "through into the ground," and Sisera never knows what hit him. As Jael looks down at the body, is she horrified at what she has done? Relieved? Triumphant?

Was Jael a cold calculating killer or a hero? In truth she was probably no more brutal then soldiers in battle. And she obviously believed the Canaanite general deserved to die, that this was a just execution. Had the Canaanites offended her in some way? Or does she simply believe the Israelites are in the right? Surely she has heard of Israel's woman judge. Does this help sway her, believing as she does, that Deborah is a righteous judge with the Lord on her side?

While Sisera is being killed by a woman, another woman awaits his return: the mother who gave him birth. "Why does his chariot delay in coming? Why do the hoof beats of his chariots tarry?" For a moment we feel for this mother who we know will never see her son again. But then she and her women talk of plunder being taken.

"Are they not finding, are they not dividing the spoil?
A maiden, two maidens for every warrior;
To Sisera a spoil of dyed work,
A spoil of dyed work embroidered,
Dyed work of double embroidery on the neck of the spoiler?"

Our sympathy fades as Barak, who has pursued Sisera and perhaps suspects that he might have headed for Heber's tent, arrives. Jael is waiting and calmly invites him in, "Come, and I will show you the man whom you are seeking." Barak enters with her and even this hardened soldier is astounded to "behold Sisera lying dead with the tent peg in his temple."

Once Sisera and his army are destroyed, the Canaanite king Jabin is soon overcome and the Israelites win their freedom. "And the land was undisturbed for forty years."

Were Deborah and Jael acquainted? Did they meet afterwards with Deborah thanking Jael for what she did? One can imagine the two women meeting and exchanging stories of their triumphs, Deborah listening approvingly as Jael relates the story of Sisera's death.

Deborah will pay tribute to Jael in the Song of Deborah and Barak, a poetic form of the story:

"Most blessed of women is Jael,
The wife of Heber the Kenite;
Most blessed is she of women in the tent."

Nor is Deborah shy about lauding her own achievements. Israel was in bad shape
"Until I, Deborah, arose,
Until I arose, a mother in Israel."

Both Deborah and Jael are tough, even merciless women who stoically do whatever they think necessary to protect their people. They may not be the kind of women you'd want to meet, but they were the kind you'd want to defend you. And for the Israelites these two women were indeed the heroes of the day.

JEPHTHAH: HUMAN SACRIFICE AND AN UNINVOLVED GOD

> When Jephthah returned home after the war,
> there was his daughter coming out to meet him,
> dancing and playing the tambourine. She was his
> only child.
> -Judges 11:34

The Book of Jephthah is about a man who overcomes adversity to achieve great success, the foolish and terrible vow he makes, and the haunting absence of God.

Jephthah begins life in the town of Gilead as the illegitimate son of a prostitute. His father acknowledges him and has him brought up with his other sons. But Jephthah's half-brothers hate and fear him. When their father dies, they hound Jephthah out of town. "You are not going to get any inheritance in our family, because you are the son of another woman." No one in town attempted to stop their cruelty; a few even egged them on, while all the men of importance looked the other way.

> Jephthah the Gileadite was a mighty warrior.
> Judges 11:1

Jephthah flees from the persecution and settles in the land of Tob away from the tribes. With intelligence and strength of mind, the youth grows into a formidable warrior and respected leader. Prosperous and successful, he has also married and has a much-loved daughter.

Then one day Jephthah can take satisfaction in the fact that those who tossed him away like refuse now seek his help. The Israelites are at war with the Ammonites. With no leader of imagination or courage, they are losing. Jephthah's reputation has grown and now the elders of Gilead visit him with a proposition.

"Come, be our commander, so we can fight the Ammonites." And we will make you our leader.

Jephthah reminds them of the abuse and derision he had known growing up in Gilead. "Didn't you hate me and drive me from my father's house? Why do you come to me now, when you're in trouble?"

The elders hang their heads in shame and admit their complicity in the hardships he had known, but now they want to make amends by honoring him and choosing him as their leader. "We are turning to you now; come with us to fight the Ammonites, and you will be our head over all who live in Gilead."

Yet Jephthah still doesn't trust them. "Suppose you take me back to fight the Ammonites." And I am victorious, "will I really be your head?"

"The elders of Gilead replied, 'The Lord is our witness; we will certainly do as you say."

"So Jephthah went with the elders of Gilead, and the people made him head and commander over them."

A Vow I Cannot Break

Now he will fight the Ammonites and win. Or will he? At first Jephthah tries to negotiate with their king which proves futile. The Ammonite king only becomes more arrogant thinking Jephthah weak. Jephthah begins to doubt himself. He has fought many a battle, but this enemy is exceptionally powerful. What if he loses? He will be disgraced before the people of his youth. And because he cannot bear the thought of such shame, Jephthah makes a vow to God, a bargain really. If the Lord will grant him victory then whatever comes toward him from his house "when I return in triumph from the Ammonites will be the Lord 's, and I will sacrifice it as a burnt offering."

Jephthah assumes of course that it will be a goat or a sheep. Animal sacrifice was still practiced in the belief that this was what God wanted. At one time human sacrifice—as horrific as it sounds to us—was an accepted practice, including the sacrificing of children.

But God had made clear when Abraham was about to kill Isaac that humanity was to move past such rituals; although it had been God himself who had cruelly demanded that Abraham kill his own son to prove his obedience and loyalty. But just as Abraham is about to strike Isaac with his knife, the more advanced side of God stays his hand.

Other cultures had equivalent stories. For the Greeks there was Agamemnon, king of Mycenae and commander of the Greek forces during the Trojan War. He and his fleet have set sail when suddenly the winds die away, leaving his ships becalmed on the ocean. A seer claims that an angry goddess is the cause of their troubles. It seems that Artemis has taken offense at Agamemnon's boast that he is a better hunter than she is, and the ruthless goddess will only be appeased if Agamemnon's daughter Iphigenia is sacrificed to her. At first Agamemnon refuses, but as his ships continue to remain trapped, he finally agrees and sends Iphigenia to her death.

Jephthah takes place long after Abraham so we would expect human sacrifice to be long gone.

He Did to Her as He had Vowed

> After the two months, she returned to her father
> and he did to her as he had vowed.
> -Judges 11:39

Jephthah does triumph over the Ammonites and is returning home elated. As he approaches his dwelling "who should come out to meet him but his daughter, dancing to the sound of tambourines!" He stops cold as he remembers the promise he made to God. Is he truly going to make of his only child, his beloved daughter a burnt offering?

Although he tears his clothes in agony and cries "Oh! My daughter, you have made me miserable and wretched, because I have made a vow to the Lord that I cannot break," Jephthah is nevertheless determined to hold fast to his vow. For Jephthah, a vow was considered sacred and to break it was an abomination worse than killing ones own child.

The daughter, who is nameless, is, astonishingly, in full agreement. Although tearful, she gives her approval, "My father, you have given your word to the Lord. Do to me just as you promised, now that the Lord has avenged you of your enemies, the Ammonites." There is no mother; she seems to have died, so there is no one else to protest.

The daughter asks for one thing only. "But grant me this one request. Give me two months to roam the hills and weep with my friends, because I will never marry."

"You may go," Jephthah tells her. "And he let her go for two months. She and the girls went into the hills and wept because she would never marry. After the two months, she returned to her father and he did to her as he had vowed."

82

Did Jephthah really kill his daughter? There are no details of how or when he did it, but the words "and he did to her as he had vowed," would indicate that he did indeed kill his daughter.

Where Was God?

The stories of Iphigenia and Jephthah's daughter were so disturbing to subsequent generations that alternative endings were devised. Iphigenia is saved at the last moment by the goddess Artemis herself who whisks her away to an island. In the case of Jephthah's daughter, some have interpreted the words to mean that she was dedicating her life to God rather than dying, somewhat like a nun. But the original ending seems more likely.

The story of Jephthah's Daughter is perhaps even more disturbing than that of Iphigenia. There you have a vengeful goddess, one who does not have any claim to morality. But Abraham's God had progressed to a new level and with him humanity. So where is God when Jephthah "did to her as he had vowed?" Why did not God stay Jephthah's hand as he did Abraham's? God's absence is haunting: has He backslid from the God of Abraham, who at the last minute could see the light that human sacrifice was not proper?

SAMSON, UNHOLY HOLY MAN

> You will become pregnant and have a son whose
> head is never to be touched by a razor.
> -Judges 13:5

When it comes to casual violence, today's action flicks have nothing on the story of Samson. For this celebrated strongman, killing a lion with his bare hands or wiping out one-thousand Philistines was all in a day's work.

Birth Announcement

As the tale of Samson begins, the Israelites have been suffering under the yoke of the Philistines for forty years because they "did evil in the eyes of the Lord," meaning they were worshipping other gods. But the Lord is about to send them a deliverer by working some of his signature reproductive magic on a childless couple.

Manoah and his wife (one of the many nameless women of the Bible) have despaired of ever having a child when the wife is approached by a stranger. "You are barren and childless, but you are going to become pregnant and give birth to a son." Needless to say, the wife is taken aback. Later she will tell her husband, "He looked like an angel of God, very awesome." The wife is full of wonderment for the angel had told her that

84

her son "will take the lead in delivering Israel from the hands of the Philistines."

He also gave me strict instructions regarding our child's upbringing, she tells her husband, even before his birth. "Now then, drink no wine or other fermented drink and do not eat anything unclean, because the boy will be a Nazirite of God from the womb until the day of his death." After he is born, the angel continued, you will see to it, that his "head is never to be touched by a razor." Nazirites were a sect dedicated to God with strict rules of conduct, including abstaining from wine and keeping one's hair uncut.

Manoah wants to believe, but still has reservations so he prays to God. "Pardon your servant, Lord. I beg you to let the man of God you sent to us come again to teach us how to bring up the boy who is to be born." God listens and once more sends his angel, who seems to prefer the wife to the husband, for he materializes when she is alone in the field. "He's here," the wife cries, running to her husband, "the man who appeared to me the other day!"

Quickly before the stranger can disappear, "Manoah got up and followed his wife." The angel confirms for the husband everything the wife had said. Manoah is thrilled at the idea of fatherhood, although he can't yet accept that their visitor is actually a messenger from God. Manoah offers to prepare a meal for the angel. The angel declines, but says a burnt offering to the Lord would be most welcome.

"Then Manoah took a young goat, together with the grain offering, and sacrificed it on a rock to the Lord." This is God's opportunity to put on a spectacular show and remove any remaining doubts the couple might have. "The Lord did an amazing thing while Manoah and his wife watched: as the flame blazed up from the altar toward heaven, the angel of the Lord ascended in the flame."

Manoah trembles. "We are doomed to die; we have seen God!" But his more commonsensical wife points out that, "If the Lord had meant to kill us, he would not have accepted a burnt offering and grain offering from our hands, nor shown us all these things or now told us this."

In the months to come Manoah and his wife fulfill the angel's words and have a son they name Samson.

I Want Her

> Samson went down to Timnah and saw there a
> young Philistine woman.
> -Judges 14:1

After the lighthearted birth story, the tale turns toward comic book style action. Samson is brought up in the strict tradition of the Nazirite sect. But as he reaches manhood, it soon becomes apparent that although he may adhere to the sect's rules such as not cutting his hair, he isn't very spiritual or wise. But he is definitely strong.

When he is old enough, Samson decides he wants to see a bit of the world outside of the tribal orbit. The enemy Philistine cities hold the most appeal for him, perhaps because they seem the most exotic and forbidden, or is it God doing a bit of manipulating? Samson winds up in the Philistine city of Timnah where he catches sight of a lovely, young Philistine woman. Without much thought, the youthful strong man decides on the spot that she's the one for him. Upon returning home he immediately informs his parents that he has met the woman of his dreams. "I have seen a Philistine woman in Timnah; now get her for me as my wife."

His parents are dismayed at their son's choice. "Isn't there an acceptable woman among your relatives or among all our people? Must you go to the uncircumcised Philistines to get a wife?"

Samson doesn't try to persuade them in calm, respectful tones; he simply and rather rudely orders his father to "Get her for me. She's the right one for me."

Maybe as a long awaited only child, Samson has been spoiled and now expects to be given whatever he wants. As it turns out, Samson's hasty bride selection is "from the Lord." God seems to be maneuvering Samson into a confrontation with the Philistines by using his propensity for easily falling in love.

His parents relent and all three travel to Timnah. While his parents are taking a rest, Samson goes off on his own. "Suddenly a young lion comes roaring toward him." We are definitely in Hercules-like legend here. Samson "tears the lion apart with his bare hands as he might have torn a young goat." So amazed is the youth at his own incredible feat that he cannot talk about it to his parents.

Once in Timnah, the three go to the house of Samson's intended where Manoah speaks with the girl's father. He is agreeable to a marriage between his daughter and Samson, and plans for the wedding celebration are made. The wedding will take place in Timnah at the bride's house because the groom's people do not approve. Even the thirty traditional groomsmen must be Philistines for no Israelite will take part.

A Riddle of Honey

Some days later, Samson and his parents are returning to Timnah for the wedding when on his own, Samson comes across the carcass of the lion he had killed, now swarming with bees and honey. Samson scoops out some of the honey and eats, and takes the rest to his parents.

The three arrive at the bride's house and the celebration commences. Several hours later, Samson turns to his groomsmen, "Let me tell you a riddle," he says.

"Out of the eater, something to eat;

out of the strong, something sweet."

"If you can give me the answer within the seven days of the feast, I will give you thirty linen garments and thirty sets of clothes. If you can't tell me the answer, you must give me thirty linen garments and thirty sets of clothes."

There is no way to guess this absurd riddle, unless you have witnessed the honey in the lion that Samson killed. Yet still the groomsmen try. For three days they desperately rack their brains for an answer, and then decide it's time to pay a visit to Samson's bride. If she doesn't wheedle the answer out of her husband, they threaten "we will burn you and your father's household to death. Did you invite us here to rob us?"

Why doesn't Samson's wife tell her husband about the threats? Does she fear her countrymen more than Samson's abilities? It may be that Samson's extraordinary strength is not yet well-known. Putting on a good act, Samson's bride quickly runs to her husband crying "You hate me! You don't really love me. You've given my people a riddle, but you haven't told me the answer."

Samson objects that he hasn't even told his own parents, "so why should I explain it to you?" That of course doesn't satisfy her and she sobs bitterly for the whole seven days of the feast." Finally, toward the end of the seventh day, Samson is worn out and reveals the answer. She promptly gives it to the groomsmen.

Not an hour passes before the groomsmen surround Samson with the words:

"What is sweeter than honey?

What is stronger than a lion?"

Revenge as God's Plan

Naturally Samson guesses that they got to his wife. "If you had not plowed with my heifer, you would not have solved my riddle." In a fine fury Samson rushes down to another Philistine city, Ashkelon, kills thirty Philistines, takes their clothing and throws the garments at the riddle solvers. The Bible tells us that Samson did all this because "the Spirit of the Lord came upon him." Who were the Philistines that Samson kills? Were they related to the groomsmen or where they simply innocent bystanders? Samson is less a real human being than a puppet in the hands of a vengeful God.

Still enraged, Samson goes back to his parents' house. But soon he starts longing for his wife and returns to the town of Timnah for her. Has Samson forgiven his wife? Does he truly want her back because he misses her? Or is this one more instance of God pulling the strings, engineering one more bloodbath?

God gets his wish when Samson discovers that his wife has been given as a bride to one of the evil groomsmen. Her father protests: "I was so sure you thoroughly hated her that I gave her to your friend. Isn't her younger sister more attractive? Take her instead."

But Samson has no desire for his wife's sister. What he does desire is revenge. "This time I have a right to get even with the Philistines; I will really harm them." Does this mean that Samson feels a bit guilty at killing the previous thirty Philistines for their clothing? Or does he feel their deaths were too merciful?

He certainly has no compunction about excessive cruelty to animals. He goes out, catches three hundred foxes, ties them tail to tail in pairs and affixes a torch to every pair of tails. Then he lights the torches and lets the pain-wracked animals loose in the Philistine grain fields, olive groves, and vineyards to destroy all the crops.

"Who did this," ask the Philistines, and are told it was Samson, "because his wife was given away."

What happens next is virtually inexplicable. Instead of going after Samson, the Philistines take revenge on Samson's poor wife "and burn her and her father to death." This is a terribly cruel act and the question of whether this too was part of God's plan arises. Or were these two lives simply too insignificant and therefore expendable in the larger picture?

The reprisals continue when Samson, hearing the news about his wife and her father, goes on a slaughtering spree. It is hard to know whether Samson truly mourns his wife or just likes to kill.

Even strongmen have to take breaks from time to time, however, and after these non-stop action sequences, Samson goes to hide and rest in a cave. But not for long.

By now Samson has become number one on the Philistines' most wanted list. Taking no chances, they send out an entire army to capture him. Spreading themselves over the land of the tribe of Judah where Samson's cave is located, they raid a nearby town as they wait. The people of Judah are disturbed and frightened and send a delegation to the Philistines asking them what they want.

"We have come to take Samson prisoner," they answer, "to do to him as he did to us." Hearing this, the people of Judah become angry at Samson. Going down to the cave, they castigate him for bringing such trouble upon them. "Don't you realize that the Philistines are rulers over us? Why have you done this to us?"

Samson's reply is an echo of the reply of his enemy: "I merely did to them what they did to me." Both sides see themselves as virtuous, and have a childish "he did it first" justification for the violence.

The men of Judah have no intention of resisting and are preparing to give the Philistines what they want. But Samson begs them not to kill him themselves but only tie him up. This they agree to and "bind him with two new ropes and lead him out of the cave."

Does Samson know something his enemies do not? You can be sure of it. When the entire Philistine army comes rushing toward him, assuming he is powerless, "the Spirit of the Lord suddenly comes upon him" and "the ropes on his arms become like charred flax, and the bindings drop from his hands." Numbly, the Philistines watch as the mighty Samson grabs the jawbone from a donkey and strikes down a full one-thousand of them.

Delilah

Samson has made fools of the Philistines. But the story isn't over. Can the Philistines exploit Samson's weakness for women?

Samson has fallen for a beautiful temptress named Delilah. She is most probably a Philistine woman but the Bible doesn't say so outright. What we know for certain is that Samson is very much in love, while Delilah is simply very greedy. When the Philistines dangle a huge reward for the secret of her lover's power, she doesn't hesitate.

Delilah goes to Samson and seductively entreats him to tell her the source of his strength. His answer: "If anyone ties me with seven fresh thongs that have not been dried, I'll become as weak as any other man."

Delilah quickly gets hold of seven fresh thongs and Samson playfully allows her to bind him. The Philistine agents are waiting to pounce, but before they emerge, Samson breaks his bonds "as easily as a piece of string snaps when it comes close to a flame."

Delilah pouts that if he really loves her he will tell her the truth. So he lets her tie him with new ropes and when that doesn't work, weave the seven braids on his head into the fabric of a loom.

Delilah persists and after several days, her lover is tiring of the game. He just cannot hold out against a woman's continuous pleadings—remember his sobbing first wife—and he gives in. "If they shave my head, my strength will vanish."

Soothingly, Delilah puts Samson "to sleep on her lap, and then summons a man to shave off the seven braids of his hair." Samson awakens to the sound of voices, jeering voices. Philistine soldiers surround him, but confident in his abilities, the strongman bolts up, ready to attack. Yet inexplicably he is like a babe, weak and helpless and unable to resist as his enemies drag him away. Then he understands, Delilah is gone, and so are his braids! We hear no more of Delilah or whether she was at all sorry for her lover's plight.

Let me die with the Philistines

Rather than kill him quickly, the Philistines decide to keep him alive, tortured and tormented. And it is here that the cartoon figure of Samson achieves a certain tragic dimension. He lies in chains, blinded, for his captors have cruelly gouged out his eyes. Samson has only one hope; that his captors will get careless. And they do.

As the days pass, Samson's jailors forget to continue shaving his head. His hair eventually grows back and unknown to the Philistines, his superhuman strength slowly returns.

One day Samson is brought into the temple of the Philistines to entertain the people. There is a great crowd with about three thousand on the roof. All the leaders and lords of the Philistines are in attendance, rejoicing and thanking their god for delivering their enemy into their hands. Great pleasure is taken at sight of the sightless, suffering Samson.

But Samson will have the last laugh. He calls out to God: "Strengthen me one last time, O Lord God, that I may get revenge upon the Philistines for the loss of my two eyes." And, bracing his arms against two pillars of the temple, he forces them outwards with all his strength. The entire building collapses with the three thousand on the roof falling upon those on the ground. And so--"in his death, Samson killed more Philistines than he had during the entire rest of his life."

The story of Samson is one of unremitting violence with a programmed killer, his weakness for women, and his puppet master god. Samson's god is Joshua's God; a god who revels in carnage.

IV. TOWARD A DYNASTY IN THE HILL TOWN OF JERUSALEM (1000 BC)

It is the prophet Samuel who anoints Israel's first monarch, Saul. He does so reluctantly and only at the behest of the people who are clamoring for a real country and a real ruler. Samuel warns them they will regret it. When they are overtaxed and burdened by rapacious kings, they will long for the days when they were free of such trappings. Samuel made a shrewd point; but there may also have been a self-interested element of 'why do you need a king when you have me and my family to lead you?'

The people refuse to listen and Saul becomes king.

MARRIED TO THE MOB: DAVID'S WIFE MICHAL

Now Saul's daughter Michal loved David.
-1 Samuel 18:20

When Michal falls in love with David, she little suspects she will become a pawn in a power struggle between two ruthless strongmen of ancient Israel. In the end, however, it is David who will prove more adept than his future father-in-law Saul - at winning friends, influencing people and cold-bloodedly removing enemies. David could have given lessons to the most skilled and brutal of Mafiosi.

The Princess, the Shepherd Boy and the Throne of Israel

When David first comes to the court of King Saul, Michal is the proud daughter of Israel's first king while David is a mere sheepherder. But the handsome youth's charm is already proving potent. Rarely does the Bible so explicitly mention a character's tender feelings; it doesn't hold back with Michal. The princess loves David passionately. Nor is Michal the only one who finds the newcomer magnetic. Michal's brother Jonathan has also become David's devoted friend while even Saul is beguiled.

What none of them know is that David is there under false pretences. According to the prophet Samuel, the youth has been slated by a wrathful God to someday replace a disobedient Saul as king. What has Saul done to merit this fate? The king has offended the Lord by sparing the life of an enemy king, Agag of the Amalekites. Saul protests that surely God should be satisfied since he killed all the rest of the enemy, but Samuel is adamant. When it comes to the worshippers of other gods, Yahweh's orders are explicit: everyone and everything must be obliterated in a kind of "cleansing" ritual. Since Saul failed at his duties, Samuel takes charge. He has the Amalekite king brought to him and "cuts Agag to pieces before the Lord at Gilgal."

Despite Saul's pleading for forgiveness, Samuel declares that "You have rejected the Lord's command, now he rejects you as king." Then the prophet hears the voice of God directing him to the house of Jesse. There he finds the new king in the person of the youngest son and anoints David then and there.

Saul Descends into Madness

> The Spirit of the Lord departs from Saul, and an evil spirit torments him.
> -1 Samuel 16:14

When David comes to work for King Saul, the priest Samuel has made David the new king--although no one knows this—and David has every intention of doing whatever is necessary to take the throne. If God, as well as Samuel, wanted a strong, ruthless man who will stop at nothing to get what he wants--the throne of Israel--then He came to the right place.

We are told that because God withdraws his support of Saul, the king's mental state begins to deteriorate and he increasingly suffers from fits of melancholy and temper. In our day, we would label him manic depressive or some other mental disorder and treat him with psychoactive drugs. The king has to make do with David's harp playing, one of the few things that can calm him down and Saul is grateful.

The king's gratitude doesn't last, however, as David's prowess in battle, along with his good looks; quickly turn him into a superhero. Women fawn over him and praises are sung in his honor, most particularly and insultingly for Saul, "David has killed his ten-thousands and Saul his one-thousand." The king takes a good long look at Israel's new celebrity and begins to see a dangerous rival, as indeed he is. Instinctively he senses the ambition, the covetousness in David regarding his throne.

Saul begins a ruthless and ultimately futile campaign to rid himself of this threat, something that will obsess him until he dies. David is sent into the thick of the most dangerous battles with the aim of getting him killed. But the young hero foils the king by winning every encounter and each time, ever more popularity.

Marry My Daughter

> I will give her to him, so that she may be a snare
> to him.
> -Samuel 18:21

Michal doesn't share her father's fears and only sees the man she loves. She has told no one yet of her feelings. But when she hears her father offering David her older sister Merab as wife, she is dismayed. Saul believes that binding David to him through marriage will provide him with plenty of murderous opportunities. David is well aware of Saul's suspicions and plots and is carefully watching every move Saul makes. Cannily he puts himself down as unworthy: "Who am I, and what is my family or my father's clan in Israel, that I should become the king's son-in-law?"

Why does David refuse? Is it because of Michal? Never does the Bible say that David loves Michal as it tells us she loves him. But he may be more attracted to her than to her sister. Moreover, he surely cannot have missed the passionate glances that Michal cannot always hide. Yes, Michal who adores him is far more appealing to David as a wife than Merab who seems to be one of the few immune to his charms.

Michal confides in her sister, begging for her help, and Merab convinces their father to use Michal for David instead. Had Saul been aware of just how devoted Michal was to David, he might have been less willing to switch daughters. But the king was a less astute observer than his future son-in-law and so had no misgivings. Happily, he makes another politically advantageous marriage for Merab, and once again asks David to be his son-in-law this time through Michal,

A Hundred Philistine Foreskins

> Then Saul gives David his daughter Michal in
> marriage.
> -1 Samuel 18:27

Now this is exactly what David wants; marrying Saul's daughter will bring him very near to the throne, but why let Saul know it. So once again he plays coy and pretends reluctance and humility, "Do you think it is a small matter to become the king's son-in-law? I'm only a poor man and little known," claiming he cannot afford the bride price. At the answer, the king exults at what he sees as a great opportunity. He will offer his rival a challenge that he cannot refuse, one that will surely prove fatal.

If David has little money, then Saul will magnanimously waive the regular bride price, asking nothing more than a hundred Philistine foreskins. If this sounds like a strange and bizarre price for a bride, it was probably no more barbaric than many tribal practices, in which body parts such as scalps were often taken as war trophies. David accepts—something he always intended to do—and stuns his future father-in-law and all of Israel when he brings back not one-hundred, but two-hundred Philistine foreskins!

So the passionately in love Michal and the coolly calculating David are married, while David's new father-in-law mulls over fresh homicidal plans.

An Idol in the Bed

Did Saul foolishly expect his daughter to meekly go along with his murderous machinations? Has his dementia made him blind to his children's affections for David? When Jonathan hears of one of his father's plots, he wastes no time in warning his friend. Then his sister, who has been keeping close tabs on her father, learns he is sending assassins to her home and hastens to tell her husband. "If you don't run for your life tonight, tomorrow you'll be killed." With Michal's help, David escapes through a window and runs for his life.

The clever princess then seeks to delay the truth from her father's agents until David is far away. She takes an idol,* puts some goat hair at the head and covers it with a garment. When her father's men arrive and ask to see David, Michal insists that her husband is ill. She allows them a glimpse of the distant figure on the bed, and the naive assassins are satisfied and leave. A less trusting Saul sends them back to bring David "so that I may kill him." But to their dismay all they find is the idol, leaving Saul furious at his guards as well as his daughter. He demands to know how she could be so disloyal and she calmly lies that she only did what she did because her husband tried to kill her.

*Note: What was an idol doing in an Israelite household? The Bible glosses over Michal's use of an idol to deceive her father. It is as if having such an item in one's home were an ordinary occurrence. Yet the first commandment explicitly states "You shall have no other gods before me." And the second is also pretty clear, "You shall not make for yourself an idol." Despite this, at the time of David (11th century BC), some Israelites routinely still kept idols.

Separation

And David takes two more wives
-1 Samuel 27:3

Saving David's life will prove a mixed blessing for Michal, for with David's escape, they are suddenly separated. It is understandable that David couldn't take Michal with him—he had to leave so quickly and Michal knew that he had a better chance if she could delay her father from finding out he was gone. But is there no way for David to send for her later even if she is watched by her father? Does he attempt to get messages to Michal? Or was she left with an unbearable silence when it came to the man she adored?

If she doesn't hear from David in the following years, Michal will certainly hear of him, painful things. She is told that David has taken two more wives and had children by them. Although having multiple wives was the custom, what Michal cannot forgive is that David seems to have totally forgotten her, his first wife. And the fact that she herself had not borne David's children hurts her unbearably.

Then a report reaches her that at first Michal refuses to believe. David is said to be a traitor! Could her husband actually have thrown in his lot with the hated Philistines? Despite David's neglect, Michal still wants to believe in David's innocence. She well knows that her father has continued his murderous pursuit; was this David's only means of saving his life?

Michal as Pawn of Strongmen

Ish-Bosheth gave orders and had her taken away
from her husband Paltiel.
-2 Samuel 3:15

Saul and David continue their mafia-style struggle for power, and Saul as a consequence decides to marry his daughter to another man, Paltiel. This will cut David completely off from the royal family, and thus eliminate any claim he might have to the throne through Michal. Does Michal object, or is she so disillusioned that she has accepted the end of her marriage and goes not unwillingly to her new husband? Fortunately, Paltiel comes to love his wife devotedly and will prove to be an anchor for her as she watches her family disintegrate.

For Michal it cannot be easy when she hears of the deaths of both her father and Jonathon at the hands of the Philistines. She mourns her beloved brother as well as her father; even though Saul's behavior was often erratic. And what next is in store for them, Michal wonders, for she well knows that her weak brother Ish-Bosheth will never be able to hold the kingdom against David. What she never expects is a white faced Paltiel coming to tell her that David is demanding Michal back again.

Husband and wife stare at each other and both realize how naive they were to think that the politically scheming David would leave them alone. Michal is still the daughter of Saul, Israel's first king; if David can use her to shore up his own claims for kingship, he will. And perhaps there is another reason why David prefers to have Michal with him and not Paltiel. For although up until now Michal has borne no children, there is no telling she might not in the future bear a son who would be Saul's grandson, and therefore a threat to David the king.

In fact a time will come when all of Saul's descendants—including the five sons of Michal's sister Merab—will be executed, although David will claim he is blameless. Deaths that benefit David seem to happen all the time – but like a good mafia boss, David's own hands will always be clean. He will always protest his innocence and grief.

Michal and Paltiel can do nothing in the face of David's demand. When Abner, David's aide, comes to escort Michal to David, the heartbroken Paltiel cannot bear to let her go, and "went with her, weeping behind her all the way to Bahurim." Finally Abner impatiently turns to Paltiel ordering him to "Go back home!" In defeat, Paltiel turns his back on his beloved Michal, never to see her again.

A Wild Dance and a Final Break

> Michal, daughter of Saul, had no children to the day of her death.
> -2 Samuel 6:23

Michal is now reunited with the man she once loved with all her heart, and there is nothing but bitterness. David has coldly torn her from the husband who cares for her, and she knows she means nothing to him--if she ever did.

David has triumphed over his enemies and is now absolute ruler of Israel. There remains only the task of bringing the ark to what is now the national as well as religious capital, Jerusalem. When that day comes, David exultantly presides over the celebrations. He arrogantly dons an ephod, a garment usually worn only by high priests during religious rites, and "dances before the Lord with all his might, while he and the entire house of Israel roll along the ark of the Lord with shouts and the sound of trumpets."

Only one person takes no part in the rejoicing. "As the Ark of the Lord was entering the City of David, Michal daughter of Saul watched from a window. And when she saw King David leaping and dancing before the Lord, she despised him in her heart."

Perhaps Michal did find the dancing distasteful and vulgar, but if she and David had been truly reconciled, it is likely that she would have been more forgiving. But has David shown her any affection whatsoever? Even if he doesn't love her, she is the woman who once saved his life and she surely deserves respect, gratitude and affection. Instead, he has ripped her away from a loving home and set her in a hostile place. Once she had been a proud princess watching her father rule, now she must watch the man who defeated her father with all his fawning women and courtiers. Does anyone show her kindness or respect? Why should they—she is only the daughter of a defeated king.

Before David can return home to bless his household, Michal runs out to meet him to pour out her venomous anger. Scornfully she questions his fitness to be king. "How the king of Israel has distinguished himself today, disrobing in the sight of the slave girls of his servants as any vulgar fellow would!"

Is there any other woman with the courage to speak to David in such a way? In a rage the king retaliates with contemptuous words about her family, "It was before the Lord, who chose me rather than your father or anyone from his house when he appointed me ruler over the Lord's people Israel-I will celebrate before the Lord. I will become even more undignified than this, and I will be humiliated in my own eyes. But by these slave girls you spoke of, I will be held in honor."

Michal knows that this is the final break. The last reference to her we have is: "And Michal daughter of Saul had no children to the day of her death." We are left to understand that David has virtually abandoned her, banished her from his presence; she will never see him again.

Could Michal have acted differently? Could she have been more subservient toward David, more flattering? Would he have been kinder to her? But Michal was a proud, outspoken woman. She could not be one of the passive court sycophants.

In the end Michal is a tragic figure, bereft of father, brothers and husband. We do not know what befalls her. We know only that David will go on to found a murderous and dysfunctional house. Perhaps Michal, distanced from the corruption and evil of the court, found, if not love, at least peace. In the end we hope so. There is a dignity and courage to Michal which stays with us long after we finish her saga.

DAVID, OUTLAW KING

> All those who were in distress or in debt or
> discontented gathered around him, and he
> became their leader.
> -1 Samuel 22:2

When David escapes a murder attempt by his wife's father Saul, he goes from being the envied son-in-law of a king to a hunted fugitive. It will be many a year before David achieves his heart's desire as supreme ruler of all Israel. In the meantime, he makes do with being king of the outlaws.

The Affair of the Holy Bread (or what can I eat?)

Eventually David will lead a formidable band of six hundred men, but now, as a lone man on the run, he must struggle with the basics of survival: food and shelter. Finding himself near the town of Nob, he seeks out Ahimelech the priest.

Ahimelech is taken aback at sight of the king's son-in-law, disheveled, dirty and obviously by himself. Nervously he asks, "Why are you alone? Why is no one with you?" David is ready with a smooth lie about a special top secret operation he's on, "The king charged me with a certain matter and said to me, 'No one is to know anything about your mission and your instructions.'" Then, to explain why he is alone, "as for my men, I have told them to meet me at a certain place." Finished with his creative explanations, David politely but firmly orders the priest to do his duty, and "give me five loaves of bread, or whatever you can find."

Ahimelech protests that he has no ordinary food on hand, only the special bread consecrated to the Lord, known as the "showbread." This food was allowed only to "men who have kept themselves from women." Quickly David insists that "indeed women have been kept from us." If

David has any compunction about lying to the priest, perhaps he feels that since he is God's anointed, the Lord will surely understand.

Table of the Showbread

If Ahimelech has any doubts, he keeps them to himself. One does not easily oppose the hero of so many battles and the king's son-in-law to boot. Quickly Ahimelech gives David what he wants and breaths a sigh of relief when he leaves.

A Consummate Actor

Once his hunger is assuaged, David must think about where he will go next. Where can he go where Saul won't find him? An audacious plan begins to form in his brain. Surely no safer place exists then in the heart of the enemy. It is the last place that Saul will look for him. Thus the Bible states quite clearly that David goes to Achish the Philistine king of Gath to offer his services. But if David is prepared to turn traitor, the Philistines aren't quite ready for him.

Naturally suspicious, they refuse to accept his vows that he will fight for them. Isn't this the man who has been so successful against us they ask, the one whose praises are sung?

> "Saul has slain his thousands,
> and David his tens of thousands'?"

And those tens of thousands he has killed are Philistines! Rather than trust him, we should kill him.

Realizing his plan has failed and seeing the menacing looks thrown his way, the ever resourceful David pulls another trick out of his hat and gives an academy award worthy performance. Slipping into the role of a madman, he suddenly begins to drool, saliva running down his beard. Clawing and scratching on the doors, his eyes darting this way and that, and muttering to himself, he convinces the court that he is a complete lunatic. Disgustedly Achish has him thrown out, declaring: "Look at the man! He is insane! Why bring him to me? Am I so short of madmen that you have to bring this fellow here to carry on like this in front of me? Must this man come into my house?"

David and his Band

David finally settles down in the forest of Hereth, and it is there that he begins to draw men to his side. First to come are his brothers and their wives and children. But then gradually "all those who were in distress or in debt or discontented gathered around him, and he became their leader." David isn't choosy, some are good men; others are the flotsam and jetsam of any society. But as long as they are willing to fight hard and ruthlessly, they are welcome. With four hundred men and growing, David is soon a force to be reckoned with, a force that Saul cannot easily defeat.

Shakedown: David, Nabal and Abigail

David and his band move into the Maon Desert near the town of Carmel where they set up a protection racket. He offers protection against thieves to those who ask for it and those who don't. Most of the people go along with it. David can be very persuasive. But the richest man in the district balks. He is Nabal, who owns a thousand goats and three thousand sheep. Nabal is described "as surly and mean in his dealings." Well he was certainly rude to David and his gang.

David's strategy in handling the difficult Nabal is to send ten strong youths to where Nabal is directing the shearing of his sheep. David sends his greetings, they call out to him: "long life to you, good health to you and your household, and good health to all that is yours!"

Their smiles are friendly, but they soon get to the heart of the matter. "Now we hear that it is sheep-shearing time. When your shepherds were with us, we did not mistreat them, and the whole time they were at Carmel nothing of theirs was missing. Ask your own servants and they will tell you."

This is more than a friendly visit. We've protected you, they assert, now we want payback. "Therefore be favorable toward us, since we come at a festive time. Please give your servants and your son David whatever you can find for them."

Nabal's eyes narrow. "Who is this David? Who is this son of Jesse?" He scoffs, "why should I take my bread and water, and the meat I have slaughtered for my shearers, and give it to men coming from who knows where?" He waves his hand in dismissal and turns his back on them.

Now Nabal may think he can oppose David, but his wife has other ideas.

Abigail Takes Charge

Abigail is a young and comely woman, who is not very satisfied in her marriage to the rich but surly Nabal. She is also smart and determined, no passive, submissive wife is she. For some time Abigail has been intrigued by tales of the dashing outlaw from her servants, several of whom have become allies of David. Now one tells her of what recently transpired.

"David sent messengers from the desert to give our master his greetings, but he hurled insults at them. Yet these men were very good to us," the servant insists. Abigail listens attentively as the servant praises the band's kindness: "the whole time we were out in the fields near them nothing was missing. Night and day they were a wall around us all the time we were herding our sheep near them."

Now because of Nabal's spiteful comments, the servant continues, David and four hundred men are about to take their revenge. You must save us he pleads, "Disaster is hanging over our master and his whole household. He is such a wicked man that no one can talk to him." Abigail quickly comes to a decision. She may be genuinely fearful of what this ruthless outlaw king will do and doubtful that Nabal can stand against him. And yet, perhaps there are other thoughts going through her head as well.

With her husband absent, Abigail has a free rein. Quickly she gives orders to have five sheep slaughtered and prepared, and to gather 200 loaves of bread, two wineskins full of wine, nearly a bushel of roasted grain, 100 clusters of raisins, and 200 fig cakes. An impressive gift indeed; the mistress is satisfied.

Abigail tells her servants to load the donkeys and go on ahead toward the hills where she knew David was living. She will follow.

David's men are armed and ready to strike while David is busy justifying his coming actions against Nabal. "It's been useless—all my watching over this fellow's property in the desert so that nothing of his was missing. He has paid me back evil for good. May God deal with David, be it ever so severely, if by morning I leave alive one male of all who belong to him!"

Abigail Meets David

Then David is told of the approaching donkeys, and the identity of the winsome woman at the rear. "As she came riding her donkey into a mountain ravine, there were David and his men descending toward her, and she met them."

Abigail sees David and he is everything she has been told, handsome, virile with a powerful aura. Compare that to her old grouch of a husband. Gracefully she alights from her donkey to fall at David's feet, her face to the ground.

"My lord, let the blame be on me alone. Please let your servant speak to you; hear what your servant has to say." Shrewdly, Abigail takes responsibility for Nabal's actions, while at the same time pointing out her husband's faults. "May my lord pay no attention to that wicked man Nabal. He is just like his name—his name is Fool, and folly goes with him. But as for me, your servant, I did not see the men my master sent."

She raises her head to meet his eyes. "Now since the Lord has kept you, my master, from bloodshed and from avenging yourself with your own hands, as surely as the Lord lives and as you live, may your enemies and all who intend to harm my master be like Nabal."

Pointing to the donkeys loaded with goods, Abigail gives David a pleading smile. "And let this gift, which your servant has brought to my master, be given to the men who follow you."

She is profuse in her admiration, "Please forgive your servant's offense, for the Lord will certainly make a lasting dynasty for my master, because he fights the Lord's battles."

And she is clever in her arguments against his attacking her household. "When the Lord has done for my master every good thing he promised concerning him and has appointed him leader over Israel, my master will not have on his conscience the staggering burden of needless bloodshed or of having avenged himself."

David is so great, the Lord will surely reward him, so great he can be merciful, so great; he need not be petty in taking vengeance.

David is impressed by her intelligence as well as her beauty. "Praise be to the Lord, the God of Israel, who has sent you today to meet me. May you be blessed for your good judgment and for keeping me from bloodshed this day and from avenging myself with my own hands. Otherwise, as surely as the Lord, the God of Israel, lives, who has kept me from harming you, if you had not come quickly to meet me, not one male belonging to Nabal would have been left alive by daybreak."

He accepts her gracious offerings and tells her to "Go home in peace. I have heard your words and granted your request." The words are simple but there is a wealth of meaning in the look he gives her.

A Convenient Death

When Abigail returns home she finds that Nabal has thrown a party celebrating in the conviction that he has gotten the better of the impudent outlaw king. "He was in high spirits and very drunk. So she told him nothing until daybreak."

In the morning, when her husband has sobered up, Abigail tells him what she has done. Did he shout at her, threaten to beat her? Did she calmly defend herself asserting that it was she who had saved the household? All the Bible tells us is that Nabal's "heart failed him and he became like a stone." Obviously the man had a heart attack or a stroke from shock. For ten days Nabal hangs on and then dies.

"When David heard that Nabal was dead, he said, 'Praise be to the Lord, who has upheld my cause against Nabal for treating me with contempt. He has kept his servant from doing wrong and has brought Nabal's wrongdoing down on his own head.'"

Nabal's death was convenient for everyone except Nabal. It kept David from committing a sin of violence—just in case David was tempted even after his promise to Abigail. And it freed his wife to make a union more to her liking.

Soon after Nabal is buried, David sends his servants to Abigail with a message: "David has sent us to you to take you to become his wife." And "Abigail quickly got on a donkey and, attended by her five maids, went with David's messengers and became his wife."

This may not have been a match made in heaven, but it was a very satisfactory one for both parties. David married a rich, well-connected widow who as an added bonus, had wit and beauty. And Abigail got a husband, who if he played his cards right, would someday be the King of Israel. She had no illusions about this being a love match. David was too much of an egotist to love any woman. Unlike Michal she had no intention of having her heart broken. But she was well content with the choice she had made. She had married the charismatic outlaw king, a very good bargain.

SUMMONING UP THE DEAD: THE WITCH OF ENDOR, KING SAUL, AND AN UNDERGROUND ADVISOR

> And no one will commit child sacrifice anymore, nor employ pagan divination, nor soothsayers nor enchanters, sorcerers, charmers, or ghost or spirit consultant or one who dabbles in black magic. -Deuteronomy 18:10

When the King of Israel decides he needs some services of the supernatural sort, naturally he gets the best: the witch of Endor.

King Saul's mental state, already precarious, suffers a severe blow when the prophet Samuel dies. It was the prophet who as Israel's spiritual leader had anointed Saul as king. Saul looked upon Samuel as his wise counselor and direct line to God. Even though Samuel had withdrawn his favor from the king, Saul still felt anchored--through his presence on earth. With the prophet's death the king feels completely bereft of guidance.

Now Saul feels like a lost child as he prepares to fight yet another battle with Israel's dreaded enemy. "When Saul sees the camp of the Philistines, he is afraid and his heart trembles greatly." He tries to communicate with God, but "the Lord does not answer him, either by dreams or by prophets."

Saul Turns to the Dark Side

With his world disintegrating around him, Saul desperately turns to a forbidden practice. He tells his two close confidants to "Seek for me a woman who is a medium that I may go to her and inquire of her." Ironically practices such as calling up the dead and foretelling the future had been banned by Saul himself at the direction of the priests who called them abominations. "And Saul had removed from the land those who were mediums and spiritists."

Nevertheless the Bible is full of magical happenings. Joseph foresees the future through dreams. Moses turns his staff into a giant snake. Jesus causes a dead person to live again, and turns water into wine. Pagan Egyptian magicians were also able to turn their staffs into serpents, but although the Bible acknowledges their power as real, it deems it malevolent.

Saul has come to believe that his only hope is through magic and he doesn't care where it comes from. His men confer. Do they dare encourage the king in such a dangerous undertaking? Yet a refusal might provoke his violent temper. There is a woman in Endor, one of the men mentions, said to have amazing abilities. As soon as the king hears, he excitedly makes preparations to find the witch; perhaps there is hope after all. Taking his two trusted aides and disguising himself in peasant clothing, Saul sets out for Endor. When the little party reaches their destination, they wait till nightfall and then go forth.

At last Saul and the witch confront each other. He studies the rather ordinary looking woman doubting whether she can indeed grant his desire. His cover has worked well and she does not know who he is. But the woman can easily guess what he wants of her. Visitors come to this sorceress in the middle of the night for just one reason. Usually she denies them, knowing full well that the law of Israel will see her punished, even executed, for what it considers her wicked ways. Only rarely now does she fulfill a request and only for a friend or family.

But as the witch eyes the tall, imposing figure, her curiosity is aroused. He is dressed in a poor man's clothing, yet he has a commanding presence. Keeping his face hidden, Saul tells her he needs her help. He has heard that there is no one better than she. "Conjure up for me, please, and bring up for me whom I shall name to you." Despite the compliment, the woman refuses, reminding him of the punishment lying in wait for anyone committing such a crime. "Behold, you know what Saul has done, how he has cut off those who are mediums and spiritists from the land. Why are you then laying a snare for my life to bring about my death?"

The disguised king assures her that "As the Lord lives, no punishment shall come upon you for this thing." Moreover he will give her whatever she asks. Now the witch is intrigued. Who does he want her to bring up she wonders and why. Is it for greed, for fear, for love? She has seen and heard it all. But when Saul directs her to "bring up Samuel for me," even she is taken aback. Samuel, Israel's illustrious late prophet? She can feel herself inching forward toward accepting the challenge. Still she remains silent. Not until the king pricks her professional pride musing out loud whether she is truly as gifted as he has heard, does she agree.

The Medium and the Message

The witch of Endor goes to work. Exactly what she does, the Bible doesn't say, but whatever it is, it has results. For suddenly the woman cries out that she sees the deceased prophet. And the spectral appearance instantly triggers recognition of the true identity of her customer. Angrily she turns to him, "Why have you deceived me? For you are Saul."

The king frantically tries to soothe her, knowing that this is his one chance to talk to the dead prophet, his last hope. "Do not be afraid; but what do you see?" Her own curiosity piqued, she stares at the approaching figure. "I see a divine being coming up out of the earth." Saul demands details so that he can confirm that it is definitely Samuel, and the witch tells him that "an old man is coming up, and he is wrapped with a robe"

Surely an old man in a robe could be anyone, but Saul is convinced that the prophet has indeed returned, and "he bows with his face to the ground and does homage." Is it truly Samuel or is Saul so distraught that he will believe anything?

Saul bows before Samuel

Now the ghostly figure talks: "Why have you disturbed me by bringing me up?" The king beseeches the prophet to help him. "I am greatly distressed; for the Philistines are waging war against me, and God has departed from me and no longer answers me, either through prophets or by dreams; therefore I have called you, that you may make known to me what I should do."

Now if Saul has thought to get help and sympathy from a dead Samuel when he had rarely gotten it from a live Samuel, he is to be bitterly disappointed. Certainly the prophet had always been hard on the king and now that he's a spirit he hasn't changed. Irritably he answers, "Why then do you ask me, since the Lord has departed from you and has become your adversary?" And mentioning Saul's rival, Samuel twists the knife in the wound declaring that "the Lord has torn the kingdom out of your hand and given it to your neighbor, to David."

Worse is to come as Samuel proclaims almost with relish the king's fate: "The Lord will also give over Israel along with you into the hands of the Philistines, therefore tomorrow you and your sons will be with me. Indeed the Lord will give over the army of Israel into the hands of the Philistines!"

The ghostly prophet is done, ready to return to his resting place, uncaringly leaving Saul in shock. Poor Saul, not only has he heard words of doom for himself, his children, and his army, but he is weak from hunger having been too anxious to eat since the day before. He collapses to the floor with no strength or will to get up.

The Séance is over: Veal Cutlets and Fresh Bread

The witch stares down at the prostrate suffering Saul. She has hated this king ever since his outlawing of practitioners of magic such as herself, but now she feels compassion for this flawed but tragic figure. Saul did not after all ask to be king, but was commanded to be so by Samuel on God's orders. Then the prophet rejects Saul when he makes a mistake that, according to Samuel, God deems unforgivable. After winning a battle, Saul allowed an enemy king to live, instead of killing everyone as the Lord apparently wanted. Then as further alienation, he took the spoils and divided it among his men, feeling that they deserved it for their efforts.

This was a grievous sin according to Samuel; the enemy that worships other gods must be totally annihilated, from people to possessions. So unpardonable is Saul's "sin" that Samuel himself hacked the enemy king to death and anointed another, David.

Now the story turns from the ghoulish to the gastronomic as the kindly witch takes pity on the king and urges him to eat. "I pray thee, hearken thou also unto the voice of thy handmaid, and let me set a morsel of bread before thee; and eat, that thou mayest have strength, when thou goest on thy way." Saul shakes his head, whispering "I will not eat." But his men and the witch keep encouraging him and ever so slowly he gets up from the ground and sits down on the bed.

Quickly the woman arranges a meal, as skillful at cooking as she is at sorcery. "She takes flour, and kneads it, and does bake unleavened bread thereof." Then taking the fatted calf she has in the house, she expertly kills it and roasts the meat. Even Saul perks up slightly at the delicious smells. "And she brought it before Saul, and before his servants; and they did eat."

Saul Faces up to his Fate

Saul has now lost all hope, knowing that tomorrow will bring his death. But in accepting his fate, a calmness has descended, and he takes small comfort in the witch's kindness to him. When they are done eating, Saul thanks the woman and they leave.

Was the witch of Endor genuine? Could she really summon up the dead from under the earth? Or was she a fraud? Did she and Saul both believe if mistakenly in her powers? Does the king truly hear Samuel's words of doom or does he hear the words that deep down he knows Samuel would utter?

Was the witch of Endor an evil woman? The Israelite priests certainly saw her that way. But what exactly were her crimes? Did she use her powers to hurt people? Certain banned practices were clearly abhorrent such as child sacrifice. Or was it simply that powers of divination were reserved for the priests and the prophets who we're told derived their abilities from God and the witch of Endor was not one of these?

The next day King Saul goes into battle knowing he is going to his death. Yet still he fights bravely, holding nothing back. When the witch of Endor later hears of his death, does she perhaps pause for a moment of silence, to commemorate this brave, tormented king?

CHILDREN OF THE MOB: DAVID'S SONS AND DAUGHTERS
PART 1: TAMAR AND HER BROTHERS: VIOLATION AND REVENGE

> And Tamar lived in her brother Absalom's
> house, a desolate woman.
> -2 Samuel 13:20

David may have been Israel's greatest king, and father of a powerful nation, but as father to his own children, he left much to be desired. Of the five children whose stories the Bible gives us, four came to terrible ends.

David's Daughter of Sorrow

David had many offspring by his numerous women, both wives and concubines. So many women and so many sons and daughters did the king have that the Bible stopped counting or naming them. Only five of his children are given to us in detail. Of these, only one is a daughter, and she is the one her father fails the most.

Like the king, Tamar is beautiful, intelligent and well-spoken, but with a dignity and gentleness that set her apart. Despite her high-born status, there is an unspoiled quality about her. Her mother is Maacah, daughter of a neighboring king, Talmai of Geshur. We are not told anything about

Maacah except that she had two children by David. Indeed David's wives have a habit of disappearing from the pages of the Bible as if they are irrelevant. But perhaps Maacah was a strong and loving mother, since her children seem to care deeply for one another. Princess Tamar's life is pleasant and uneventful as she waits patiently for the king to arrange a politically advantageous marriage. Devoted to her brother Absalom, and her fond if distant father, Tamar is content.

There is no reason for Tamar to suspect anything unusual when one day David calls her in and asks her to go to her sick brother Amnon's bedside. What Tamar is totally unaware of is the poison in her half-brother, a poison that has dangerously focused on her.

Amnon's Trap

> When she brought the cakes for him to eat, he
> seized her and said "Come, lie with me, my
> sister."
> -2 Samuel 13:11

Amnon is David's eldest, his father's spoiled favorite and the heir to the throne. Having been denied nothing by the king, Amnon has all of David's arrogance and none of his charm or abilities. He believes he can do whatever he pleases, never more so then when it comes to women. And why not--hasn't he watched his role model over the years take whatever woman he wants without thought?

Did his father restrain himself when he caught sight of an unknown woman bathing? No, he had his men bring her to him and when done, sent her back. Despite the fact that popular legend presents Bathsheba as David's great love, the Bible actually gives us a few stark sentences of David taking a woman without thought and certainly without permission. And when her resulting pregnancy threatens to embarrass him, the king first seeks to pass the child off as her husband Uriah's, and when that fails, he has this brave and upright soldier sent to the frontlines to be killed.

Why then should Amnon have any scruples when his eyes alight on a certain woman, even if that woman is his own half-sister? With his evil cousin Jonadab egging him on, he plots to ensnare the unsuspecting Tamar, justifying himself with the notion that he loves her. Amnon pretends to be ill and when David comes to visit he begs his father to "Please let my sister Tamar come and make me a couple of cakes in my sight, that I may eat from her hand." Does Amnon purposely bring his father into the plot to share the blame? And does David truly suspect nothing?

The sympathetic Tamar quickly goes to her brother only to find a predator lying in wait. She tries to reason with him "Don't force me. Such a thing should not be done in Israel! Don't do this wicked thing." Despite her danger, Tamar is eloquent, "What about me? Where could I get rid of my disgrace? And what about you? You would be like one of the wicked fools in Israel."

Tamar even beseeches him to speak with their father about a marriage between them! "Please speak to the king; he will not keep me from being married to you." This may sound strange, but at the time incest was common in that part of the world and perhaps not yet banned in Israel, particularly between half-siblings. But Amnon cares nothing about Tamar's arguments, much less her feelings. His only goal is to satisfy his lust. And when he's through, lest any doubt about the evil act he's committed invade his mind, he quickly turns against the innocent victim. In what must surely be one of the most horrific scenes in the Bible, Amnon screams at Tamar with hatred, "Get up and get out!"

Amazingly, Tamar still manages to speak with clarity and dignity: "No!" she said to him. "Sending me away would be a greater wrong than what you have already done to me." But the malevolent prince only turns away calling his servant to "Get this woman out of here and bolt the door."

The obedient servant does just that and when Tamar leaves the house, she knows her life has changed forever. A woman who was raped was no longer acceptable as a potential wife, therefore of what value was she now? It made no difference that she was the innocent victim. She would exist in a kind of twilight world from now on. In mourning for herself and her former life, Tamar rends her luxuriant, royal robes and puts ashes on her head.

A Father's Failure

Surely the king's weeping daughter must have been recognized as she passed by. Did those who saw her suspect what had happened? It is telling that Tamar does not go to her father for help. It is with her beloved brother that she seeks refuge and Absalom at least does not fail her. Appalled at what has happened, he makes his sister as comfortable as possible, soothing her and letting her know that she will live with him now. Yet even as Absalom comforts his sister, in the back of his mind there is another thought hovering: punishment for Amnon.

But punishment Absalom knows is properly up to the king and he awaits his father's judgment. Yet David is strangely tentative when told of the disturbing events. The Bible tells us "he is furious," surely a rather mild reaction to such a heinous crime and against his own daughter. And then what does David do? Nothing. Perhaps the king did call Amnon in and rebuke him. Did Amnon then give some excuse maybe even claiming that Tamar had tempted him? Whatever passes between father and son, David promptly forgives and forgets. This may not be the first time David has brushed off an unpleasant episode involving Amnon, for surely the young man has committed foul acts before this.

That David is as guilty as his son of what befell his daughter is inescapable. He was the one who sent Tamar to her fate. He should have known what Amnon was capable of. If David did not know, it is only because he was willfully blind. He failed to protect his innocent daughter from his violent, amoral son, a crime equal to the one perpetrated against Uriah, Bathsheba's' husband. Does David ever see his daughter afterwards? Or does he pretend she no longer exists?

When Absalom realizes that his father has no intention of punishing Amnon, he determines that his half-brother will pay no matter how long it takes. He will be patient, lulling his father and brother into thinking that all has been forgotten.

Absalom's Revenge

Absalom never said a word to Amnon, either good or bad, although he hated Amnon because he had disgraced his sister. -2 Samuel 13:22

For two years Absalom bides his time. Now he thinks, surely my father and brother will trust me. At first, David seems somewhat suspicious when Absalom invites him and all his brothers to a big feast to celebrate the sheep shearing season. "No, my son, we should not all go, for we will be burdensome to you." But Absalom persists and although David declines, "he lets Amnon and all the king's sons go with him," perhaps hoping for reconciliation in his family. Obviously, the king knew as little about Absalom's character as he did about Amnon's. Otherwise he would have known that Absalom would never forget the crime committed against his sister.

And how could Amnon not have had the sense to realize his brother's intentions? Or did he think himself safe, arrogantly assuming that Absalom would never dare harm David's darling son and heir? He is wrong, for as soon as everyone, including Amnon is "merry with wine," Absalom gives the signal and his men rush forward to stab the now terrified prince to death. Was Absalom wrong to take matters into his own hands? Yet who else would have done it once David washed his hands of the whole affair?

Absalom Escapes

Absalom does not wait to hear about his father's grief and rage. He flees at once to his maternal grandfather in Geshur. Three years pass and David's anger against Absalom is still raw. Not until the intervention of David's general Joab, does David relent a little: "All right, I'll do it. Go and bring the young man Absalom back." Yet still the king holds onto his resentment: "He may return to his house, but he is not to see me face to face." So Absalom comes home but does not see his father for another two years. David's treatment of Absalom seems unusually harsh considering he did nothing to Amnon.

Somewhere along the line Absalom decides that it isn't enough to be the king's heir. He wants to be king now. Perhaps he decided so right after David's failure to act against Amnon. Or maybe it was his father's stubborn refusal to see him even after five years that triggers Absalom's desire for the throne. Whatever the reason, he was certainly no more ambitious than David himself had been. And he could easily rationalize that his aging father is weak and corrupt, no longer fit to be king.

A Political Pro like Dad

The hearts of the men of Israel are with Absalom.
-2 Samuel 15:13

When Absalom and his father finally meet again their reconciliation is stilted, and soon the son begins to subtly challenge the father. The would-be king surrounds himself with a royal retinue, such as a "chariot and horses and fifty men to run ahead of him." Setting himself up near the city gates, he curries favor with those who are seeking the king's judgment. "What town are you from," he would smile, "your servant is from one of the tribes of Israel." And then almost with regret "Look, your claims are valid and proper, but there is no representative of the king to hear you. If only I were appointed judge in the land! Then everyone who has a complaint or case could come to me and I would see that he gets justice."

"And when a man came near to prostrate himself before him, he would put out his hand and take hold of him and kiss him." The crown prince is proving himself to be a first-rate politician, not to mention the fact that "in all Israel there was not a man so highly praised for his handsome appearance as Absalom." Once David was Israel's charismatic, good looking hero, now all the talk is of his son who "from the top of his head to the sole of his foot there is no blemish in him."

After four years, Absalom is ready for open rebellion, sending messengers throughout Israel to declare, "As soon as you hear the sound of the trumpets, then say, "Absalom is king." When David hears that his subjects are deserting him for Absalom, he weeps. Once upon a time, David would have made a strong stand, now he can only make plans to flee.

Locked Away: The Ten Widows of David

> They were kept in confinement till the day of
> their death, living as widows. -2 Samuel 20:3

The king sets out, with his entire household following him; all that is except his ten concubines who he leaves to "take care of the palace." We will never get to know these women as individuals, nor hear their voices. Up until the war between David and Absalom, their lives were no doubt as good as most women of the time and probably better. The ten lived in as much ease and luxury as time and place could offer. It is likely that several if not all had children by David. Then comes the conflict between father and son and in a short time these women will be treated as less than human, their only value as weapons of war.

Now Absalom may not have been the sexual predator his brother Amnon was, but he could be every bit as ruthless, especially toward women, as his father when it came to his ambitions. When his counselor, Ahitophel, reminds him that for a man to take the wife or mistress of a king was to lay claim to the throne of that king, he listens intently. "Lie with your father's concubines whom he left to take care of the palace, then all Israel will hear that you have made yourself a stench in your father's nostrils, and the hands of everyone with you will be strengthened."

In a primitive, animal-like ritual, in the way a victorious male lion conquers his rival's harem, Absalom can declare his power, his dominance over his father. "So they pitched a tent for Absalom on the roof, and he lay with his father's concubines in the sight of all Israel." One by one these women come to him, silent, accepting of their fate. Each is nothing more than a means by which Absalom can demonstrate to David and all Israel that he is supreme.

A Father's Grief

It might have been better for the ten women had Absalom won, it surely couldn't have been worse. But Absalom is not lucky enough or perhaps clever enough to succeed. By not striking when his father was weak, he allows David to find the spark to energize his forces. In the ensuing battle Absalom is killed.

David had ordered his men to "be gentle with the young man Absalom for my sake." And when he hears that his son is dead, he is shocked and genuinely heartbroken. Weeping, he utters his heartrending cry "O my son Absalom! My son, my son Absalom! If only I had died instead of you—O Absalom, my son, my son!" Does David now have some sense of his own guilt in the tragedies that have befallen his family?

Whatever his grief for his son, it does not soften his attitude toward his now tainted women. "He took the ten concubines he had left to take care of the palace and put them in a house under guard. He provided for them, but did not lie with them. They were kept in confinement till the day of their death, living as widows."

Whatever affection David may once have felt toward them, they have now been touched by another man and are no longer fit to belong to him. One might say that the king was merciful in not putting them to death, but merely locking them away forever. Are they locked in together? Do they ever see their children or the outside world? It is possible that under such conditions, they did not survive for very long.

PART 2: THE LUCKY AND THE UNLUCKY: SOLOMON AND ADONIJAH

> Now Adonijah put himself forward and said, "I will be king."
> 1 Kings 1:5

> Our lord King David has made Solomon king.
> 1 Kings 1:43

With the death of Absalom, David's two other sons, Adonijah and Solomon, now move up the line of succession. Of course Adonijah is the elder and so is first in line. Or so he thinks.

But if Solomon was wise, he was also lucky enough to have the support of a key prophet, Nathan, a clever, energetic mother, and his father's approval, something neither Absalom nor Adonijah had. Without this luck, along with the ruthlessness he shares with his father, the young prince might never have gotten the opportunity to become Solomon the Wise.

After Absalom's death, David gradually loses the temporary spurt of energy that had sustained him in the war with his son. Gradually he becomes too weak and frail to even keep warm and his courtiers rack their brains to relieve his suffering since no amount of clothing seems to help. What about human warmth suggests one and immediately a search is instituted for a nurse who can also provide body heat. But not just any old nurse will do, for although the king is too weak at this point to need the services of a mistress, the woman who attends to his health needs is still required to be young, beautiful and virginal. Abishag the Shunammite fits the bill and becomes David's caregiver.

Watching his father as he deteriorates, Adonijah begins to garner support for his cause. Unfortunately for the young man, he has made an enemy of Nathan, David's powerful prophet. What happened between them we don't know, but as Adonijah gains in popularity, Nathan decides to have a talk with Solomon's mother, Bathsheba.

Nathan Plots with Bathsheba

Nathan quickly gets to the point, asking if she's heard that Adonijah is ready to set himself up as king. Their eyes meet in perfect agreement, Adonijah must be stopped. Bathsheba goes at once to David's bedside; and bowing low, kneels down and says the words she and Nathan have agreed upon.

"My lord, you yourself swore to me your servant by the Lord your God: Solomon your son shall be king after me, and he will sit on my throne." Not until now have we heard that David had previously intended his youngest son to succeed him. Certainly he had once seemed to expect Amnon to follow him. But either David has changed his mind in the interim or Bathsheba and Nathan are hoping to implant this suggestion in a mind gone frail.

Bathsheba asserts that Adonijah has gone behind the king's back and already set himself up as king. Strictly speaking, this is untrue; Adonijah is certainly lobbying to become king but has not already done so. And finally Bathsheba ends with "My lord the king, the eyes of all Israel are on you, to learn from you who will sit on the throne of my lord the king after him. Otherwise, as soon as my lord the king is laid to rest with his fathers, I and my son Solomon will be treated as criminals."

At that moment, Nathan arrives just as the two had planned, to drive home Adonijah's disrespect for his father. "Have you, my lord the king, declared that Adonijah shall be king after you, and that he will sit on your throne?" Sick as he is, David's anger is inflamed with the news (according to Nathan) that Adonijah is at this moment celebrating with ungrateful courtiers and shouts of "Long live King Adonijah!"

Is this what the king wants, Nathan turns the screw: "Is this something my lord the king has done without letting his servants know who should sit on the throne of my lord the king after him?"

A spark of anger rouses the fragile monarch. Adonijah shall not get the better of me he vows. And before Nathan and Bathsheba, David swears that "Solomon shall be king after me, and he will sit on my throne in my place." Well satisfied, Bathsheba bows and blesses the king: "May my lord King David live forever!"

Adonijah is indeed celebrating with his supporters and was indeed guilty of wanting to be king. But he was certainly no more ambitious than Solomon and his mother were and David had been. Adonijah's party soon turns into a fiasco as a messenger arrives to reveal that "Our lord King

David has made Solomon king," having had him anointed by Nathan the prophet. "And the king bowed in worship on his bed and said, 'Praise be to the Lord, the God of Israel, who has allowed my eyes to see a successor on my throne today.'"

Adonijah's guests hurriedly desert him for safer territory. The prince himself understands that for now at least all is lost and prudently goes to his brother the new king, and swears loyalty. Solomon seemingly agrees that if his brother "shows himself to be a worthy man, not a hair of his head will fall to the ground."

A Father's Deathbed Advice

> The new ruler must determine all the injuries
> that he will need to inflict. He must inflict them
> once and for all.
> -Niccolo Machiavelli

> Bring his gray head down to the grave in blood.
> -David on his deathbed to his son Solomon
> (1 Kings 2:9)

As David realizes the end of life is very near, he calls the new king to his side for some final words.

"Observe what the Lord your God requires: Walk in his ways, and keep his decrees and commands, his laws and requirements, as written in the Law of Moses, so that you may prosper in all you do and wherever you go."

Then, with godly rules taken care of, David goes on to thoughts of vengeance, which give him a sudden strength. These are the people he wants eliminated after he dies, the king tells his son. First there is Joab, his nephew and longtime general and counselor, who David feels, wrongly killed two men. "Deal with him according to your wisdom, but do not let his gray head go down to the grave in peace.

Next is Shimei, who had supported Absalom and as a member of Saul's clan had cursed David for "all the blood you shed in the household of Saul, in whose place you have reigned." When David emerged victorious, Shimei had begged for forgiveness and the king, supposedly showing his merciful side had promised that "You shall not die." But the crafty David had only sworn that he himself wouldn't do the deed. Now that he is dying—and still bearing a grudge—he can have his son do the dirty work when he is gone. So he says to Solomon "you are a man of wisdom; you will know what to do to him. Bring his gray head down to the grave in blood."

Solomon listens attentively to his father's speech and nods. Satisfied that his son will do all he asks, David allows death to take him.

Adonijah the Fool?

Following David's death, Adonijah goes to Bathsheba with a strange request regarding David's young and beautiful nurse: "Please ask King Solomon—he will not refuse you—to give me Abishag the Shunammite as my wife." An insignificant request? Hardly, since as we have seen with Absalom, for a man to take the wife or mistress of a king (and although Abishag never officially became David's mistress, she was still considered his woman) was to lay claim to the throne. So why would Adonijah make such a request, knowing that Solomon would rightly take it as a threat? Was he stupid or mad? Or was there some plot afoot?

There is no mention of any plot, no evidence of insanity and it is hard to believe that a son of the wily David could be so stupid. So the question is, did Adonijah really make such a request? Or was the story a fabrication of Solomon's PR department to justify the murder of his brother, or a story created by Bathsheba?

David's Lesson for Solomon: the Seven Descendants of Saul

If Solomon needed a lesson on how to deal with threatening relatives while remaining blameless, he had no better one than what befell the descendents of his father's predecessor, King Saul. It so happened that there was a famine in the land and when David asks why, he is given a vision that God is angry on behalf of the Gibeonites, a people whom Saul once tried to destroy. Although the Gibeonites were non-Israelites, there apparently was some sort of agreement that they would not be harmed and the Lord had suspended his usual rule of destruction against those who worshipped other gods. But Saul, who never seemed to get it right, being merciful when he was supposed to be pitiless, attacked the Gibeonites when he was supposed to be peaceable.

Years later, all of Israel pays the price for Saul's stupidity when God creates a famine to get even. When David asks the Gibeonites what he can do to make amends, they tell him that all they want is "seven of his [Saul's] male descendants to be given to us to be killed." To please God and the Gibeonites, the king agrees to hand over two of Saul's sons and five of his grandsons "to the Gibeonites, who kill and expose them on a hill before the Lord." That killing Saul's descendants happened to also eliminate any potential threat to David's kingship is surely coincidental.

That Adonijah's death will do the same for Solomon is also surely by chance. Was it Solomon's fault that Adonijah has proven to be an untrustworthy character and must die for the sake of the nation?

Solomon's Agenda

"King Solomon gave orders to Benaiah son of Jehoiada, and he struck down Adonijah and he died." In truth, Solomon was no more brutal than others of his time and correct in thinking that Adonijah was a threat. It is probable that Adonijah would have challenged his brother as soon as the opportunity arose and likely would have been just as ruthless.

Solomon goes to the next item on his list, Joab. Not only did his father request that Joab die, but Solomon himself has no love for the man, since Joab had sided with Adonijah. When word reaches Joab that Solomon is cleaning house, he takes refuge at "the tent of the Lord and takes hold of the horns of the altar." But if Joab thinks this will stop Solomon, he is sadly mistaken. Solomon is sure that the Lord wants Joab to be executed because "of the innocent blood that Joab shed." So the king sends his efficient henchman, Benaiah, who "went up and struck down Joab and killed him."

There remains only Shimei, and at first it seems that he will be allowed to live. Solomon sends for the terrified man and tells him to "build yourself a house in Jerusalem and live there, but do not go anywhere else. The day you leave and cross the Kidron Valley, you can be sure you will die; your blood will be on your own head." Trembling, Shimei replies "What you say is good. Your servant will do as my lord the king has said."

So why does Shimei leave his house three years later, knowing what his fate would be? Supposedly he is told that two of his slaves have run off to Gath and Shimei goes in search of them." When he returns, a summons is waiting from the king. "Did I not make you swear by the Lord and warn you?"

Then Solomon reminds Shimei of his curses toward his father: "You know in your heart all the wrong you did to my father David. Now the Lord will repay you for your wrongdoing. But King Solomon will be blessed, and David's throne will remain secure before the Lord forever." At that the king orders the faithful Benaiah to finish off the last item on his father's list.

Note: What happens to Absalom's children? We are told that Absalom had three sons and a daughter whom he named after his sister Tamar (Sam 2:14). Yet elsewhere (Sam 18:10) Absalom mentions that "I have no son to carry on the memory of my name." Could this be a reference to the fact that at some point later on they were gotten rid of?

Solomon the Unwise

With his kingdom cleansed of enemies, Solomon settles down for a long reign and for awhile all is well. Solomon builds the temple and there is peace and prosperity in the land. Unfortunately the king has highly extravagant habits and the only way to support them is through mercilessly high taxes. Soon his 300 wives, his numerous building plans and lavish lifestyle become an intolerable burden on his people.

The king must even use conscripted labor for his construction projects, further engendering dissatisfaction among the Israelites. As the years pass, his people are reminded of what the prophet Samuel warned of (1 Samuel 8:14) when they first demanded a king a generation ago:

"He will take the best of your fields and vineyards and give them to his favorites. He will take a tenth of your grain and of your vintage and give it to his officials. He will take a tenth of your flocks, and you yourselves will become his slaves. When that day comes, you will cry out for relief from the king you have chosen, and the Lord will not answer you in that day."

Nor, we are told, does God approve of Solomon. The king of Israel has become something of a polytheist! He worships not only Yahweh, but also Astarte, Chemosh and Molech alongside his many foreign wives. It is for this reason, the Bible tells us, that God will break the promise he made to David that, "Your house and your kingdom will endure forever before me; your throne will be established forever."

Without God's support and a strong kingly personality, the kingdom splits apart after Solomon's death, never to be united again. But why must God punish all of Israel for Solomon's mistakes, particularly since the House of David was the Lord's own choice?

David and his Sons: more cold-blooded and cruel than other rulers?

Why did David have so much trouble with his sons? In one way—that of his sons' ambitions--David's troubles were not unusual, it being the nature of the beast. A king needed a son to ensure the continuation and stability of his line. But times were precarious—child mortality was high. Thus just one son wasn't enough and a king would beget as many sons as possible. Sometimes fortunately or unfortunately, as fate would prove, all the sons grew up to covet the throne, threaten their father and each other and often kill to satisfy their ambitions. But if David's problems were no worse than other kings, neither were they any better because he happened to be God's anointed. And if the brutality of David and Solomon was also on a par with the times, weren't they supposed to be better than other men?

V. ENLIGHTENMENTS: FROM WONDER WORKERS TO PRACTICAL PROPHETS (800 BC)

In 800 BC lived the prophet Elijah. He was followed by his protégé Elisha. They were practitioners of fantastical doings, raising the dead, increasing the food supply. Yet a mere century later, their kind of "magic" is gone. However, the prophets who came after were, in their way, every bit as amazing as Elijah and Elisha. For they were the advisers of morality and ethics.

WONDER WORKER ELIJAH: THE MAN WHO COULD RAISE THE DEAD

> And the boy's life returned to him, and he lived.
> -1 Kings 17:22

He can part the waters, magically increase the food supply, and raise the dead. He is Elijah, the prophet. One of a series of preachers in the period following Solomon's death, Elijah is the most mysterious, and the most powerful and yet at the same time, full of very human doubts and emotions.

We know nothing about his background, his parents, or his childhood. Not even a brief "son of" reference are we given. Only in the mention of "Elijah the Tishbite, from Tishbe" are we told something personal. Elijah makes his first appearance as a grown man, already a prophet and about to exercise his powers on the weather. "As the Lord, the God of Israel, lives, whom I serve, there will be neither dew nor rain in the next few years except at my word," he thunders to Ahab, the king of Israel.

The year is about 870 BC. The original Israelite nation is now divided into Judah, the southern kingdom, still ruled by the descendants of David, and Israel the northern kingdom. From the beginning, the northern kingdom has been led by a succession of monarchs who do "what is evil in the sight of the Lord." Now we are told, Ahab is the worst of all. Not only has he married the pagan Phoenician princess, Jezebel, who uses her influence to persecute the prophets of the Lord, but the king himself has made Baal worship official in Israel by building a temple to him.

Fed by the Ravens

In the following days and weeks, no rain falls upon Israel just as Elijah had warned, and the people begin to fear the prophet. If Ahab himself refuses to believe in Elijah's powers, he still seeks to arrest him as a troublemaker. As the prophet hastens to escape before he can be captured, he gets direct counsel from the Lord, "Leave here, turn eastward and hide in the Kerith Ravine, east of the Jordan." Once there, he is safe, and despite all their efforts, Ahab's men fail at their task.

It is a peaceful if lonely place, but Elijah is used to being alone. He is well provided for as there is water from the nearby brook, while the Lord sends a flock of ravens to supply him with food. Every morning and every evening the black birds come with bread and meat. Today ravens are often thought of as ominous birds, harbingers of death, but among the Jews and many ancient civilizations at that time they were symbols of the divine.

A Jar of Flour, a Jug of Oil and Many Good Meals

Yet even here the water eventually dries up and when it does, God instructs Elijah to go to the town of Zarephath of Sidon where "I have commanded a widow in that place to supply you with food." He finds the woman collecting sticks and she willingly shares her water with the man of God. But the famine has fallen heavily on the town, and she has almost nothing left in the way of food. With sad eyes, she reveals that with a "handful of flour in a jar and a little oil in a jug" she plans to "make a meal for us, that we may eat it—and die."

Elijah assures her that all will be well. Just use what food she has for all three of them and she will still have flour and oil left to make more. In fact he smiles "the jar of flour will not be used up and the jug of oil will not run dry until the day the Lord gives rain on the land." Naturally the widow is doubtful, but decides she has nothing to lose in humoring the confident looking gentlemen. Much to her astonishment, no matter how much flour or oil she uses up, the amount never diminishes. So Elijah stays with them and in the following days, the three have enough to eat.

A Child Dies, And Lives

The widow is full of gratitude until one day her son falls ill. As he worsens, his mother despairs, and when he dies, she rails at the prophet for giving them the means to live only to have her boy die. Stunned, Elijah lifts the child's body from the bed and carries him to his own room. Usually he can stoically accept what God has decreed, but not now. As the prophet gently lowers the boy to the bed, he cries out in anguish, "O Lord my God, why have you brought tragedy upon this widow I am staying with, by causing her son to die?" Then three times he stretches himself over the boy, each time pleading with God to "let this boy's life return to him!"

After the third time, Elijah looks down to find the child's eyes looking up at him sparkling with life. Quickly he gathers him up and returns him to his grieving mother. "Look, your son is alive!" Taking her boy, the widow cradles him close, "Now I know that you are a man of God and that the word of the Lord from your mouth is the truth."

Elijah vs. the 450 Pagan Priests of Baal

Three more years of famine and starvation pass while King Ahab continues his manhunt for the prophet he detests. When the king is told that Elijah has returned of his own free will, Ahab goes to meet his enemy and as soon as he sees him, sneers, "Is that you, you troubler of Israel?"

"I have not made trouble for Israel," Elijah counters. You and your family are the cause of Israel's suffering. "You have abandoned the Lord's commands and have followed the Baals." And now Elijah throws out a challenge. Will the king dare test his 450 priests of Baal against one lone prophet of the Lord? Ahab is taken aback and if he has any doubts he doesn't show them, but immediately agrees to send word of the coming event to the priests and all of the people of Israel.

The testing takes place on Mount Carmel, and when all of the priests have assembled, Elijah, who is not only a great prophet, but a superlative showman, addresses the watching crowds. He points to himself and then to the priests, "I am the only one of the Lord's prophets left, but Baal has four hundred and fifty prophets." Then he has two bulls brought forth. Elijah allows the priests to make the first choice and prepare their animal for sacrifice, but without lighting the fire. "Call on the name of your god, and I will call on the name of the Lord," the prophet declares. "The god who answers by fire—he is God."

The priests begin to call on their deity to set the wood on fire, "O Baal, answer us!" And they dance around their altar. Hours pass as they grow increasingly frantic at the lack of response.

"Shout louder," Elijah jeers, "for surely he is a god! Perhaps he is deep in thought, or busy, or traveling." Since "traveling" is a euphemism for going to the bathroom, this elicits a great deal of raucous laughter from the audience. Finally the priests slash themselves with swords and spears in a bloody ritual, but to no avail.

As the sun sets, the priests are exhausted and humiliated, and the people becoming ever more restless. Elijah turns to the Israelites and tells them to come near the altar of the Lord that he has built. He has laid the bull on the wood, and so they will truly understand the power of the Lord, the prophet has water poured all over the offering and the wood until they are soaked. When all is done, he prays: "O Lord, God of Abraham, Isaac and Israel, let it be known today that you are God in Israel and that I am your servant and have done all these things at your command. Answer me, O Lord, answer me, so these people will know that you, O Lord, are God, and that you are turning their hearts back again."

"Then the fire of the Lord fell and burned up the sacrifice, the wood, the stones and the soil." Chastened, the Israelites fall to the ground, crying "The Lord-he is God! The Lord-he is God!" Elijah, being well aware of the fickleness of the people, takes full advantage of their present support and orders them to seize all of Baal's priests. For the avenging prophet, there is no room for mercy, and he "has them brought down to the Kishon Valley and slaughtered there."

When Ahab hears that the priests are dead, he runs to tell his wife. As he does so, Elijah performs another miracle, ending the long drought with a heavy rainstorm. But that doesn't earn him the gratitude of either King or Queen who do not seem impressed by any of his feats. All Jezebel can think about is vengeance against the hated prophet and she sends him a threatening message: "if by this time tomorrow I do not make your life like that of one of them, may the gods deal with me, be it ever so severely."

Elijah Faces a Life Crisis

Elijah is a brave man, but he knows Jezebel is a determined woman. Suddenly the odds against him seem overwhelming, and fearfully he runs. But it isn't only fear assailing Elijah, but self-doubt. He is alone, without family or friends or home, a wanderer who has devoted himself to God's work. But what have I accomplished, he wonders. And concluding that nothing he's done has truly made a difference, he descends into a crisis of the spirit so deep that he wants to die.

Leaving civilization behind, he journeys into the desert without food or water, and coming to a tree sinks down beneath it. Elijah is mentally and physically exhausted and his last words before going to sleep are addressed to God: "I have had enough, Lord, take my life; I am no better than my ancestors."

But God has no intention of allowing his troubled prophet to die, and after first letting him get some much needed rest, sends an angel to wake him up. God's assistant orders Elijah to eat and "he looks around, and there by his head is a cake of bread baked over hot coals, and a jar of water." Much to his surprise, he enjoys the meal and when he is done, the angel tells him to go to sleep again.

After another healing sleep, he is once again awakened, and once more urged to eat and drink. This time, however, when he is finished, the next order of business is a journey. Elijah will travel for forty days and forty nights—a magical number found throughout the Bible—until he reaches Mt. Horeb, "the mountain of God."

Here God comes to him wanting to know what the problem is. And Elijah vents his frustration and bitterness. "I have been very zealous for the Lord God Almighty." But has he really done anything of value? "The Israelites have rejected your covenant, broken down your altars, and put your prophets to death with the sword. I am the only one left, and now they are trying to kill me too."

Instead of answering Elijah directly, God tells him to "Go out and stand on the mountain in the presence of the Lord, for the Lord is about to pass by."

"Then a great and powerful wind tore the mountains apart and shattered the rocks before the Lord, but the Lord was not in the wind. After the wind there was an earthquake, but the Lord was not in the earthquake. After the earthquake came a fire, but the Lord was not in the fire. And after the fire came a gentle whisper. When Elijah heard it, he pulled his cloak over his face and went out and stood at the mouth of the cave."

God has shown his suffering prophet that the divine and the good are not only to be found in the grand and spectacular but in the small and the gentle. Moreover, although Elijah may not have convinced the majority in

Israel to turn back to the Lord, there are still many thousands "whose knees have not bowed down to Baal and whose mouths have not kissed him."

Go back to the world he tells Elijah and do your work. Even small accomplishments are important. And he tells him to find and anoint the one who is meant to succeed him and who will help him now.

Elisha: Protégé, Helper and Friend

So Elijah goes back to civilization and finds the young Elisha son of Shaphat. He is plowing on his farm, when Israel's prophet goes up to him and throws his cloak around him. Elisha stops and looks at the older man. As recognition dawns, Elisha understands the meaning of the gesture, that Elijah has declared him to be his successor. At once Elisha accepts his fate. He asks only that he be allowed to "kiss my father and mother good-by, and then I will come with you."

At that Elijah has a pang of guilt at taking the young man away from his family to a life of hardship. "Go back," Elijah replied. "What have I done to you?" Of course he can take as long as he needs to make preparations and say goodbye.

The Bible tells us that before he leaves, Elisha kills his own oxen to feed the people in his village. When he is done, the young man embraces his parents and goes out to follow his new mentor. The prophet will teach Elisha all that he knows and in return, the protégé will become for Elijah like a son, sharing the burdens that the prophet has borne, up until now, alone.

Jezebel and the Vineyard

With God's words echoing in his head and Elisha by his side, Elijah's energy is renewed and he returns to the work of a prophet. It is none too soon, for Queen Jezebel is busy committing fresh crimes, one in particular against Naboth, owner of a vineyard.

This vineyard is very near to the palace and is coveted by the king. But no matter how much Ahab offers for the property, Naboth refuses to sell. "The Lord forbids that I should give you the inheritance of my fathers." This attitude doesn't sit too well with the king, and like a spoiled child, he goes home and sulks, refusing to eat. When he whines to his wife, Jezebel is scornful: "Is this how you act as king over Israel? Get up and eat! Cheer up. I'll get you the vineyard of Naboth the Jezreelite."

The queen's plan is simple. She arranges a feast in Ahab's name and invites Naboth. Sitting opposite him are two con men she has bribed to accuse the vineyard owner of "cursing both God and the king." The unfortunate Naboth protests his innocence, but despite his pleas, he is forced outside and quickly stoned to death before any doubters can raise questions.

Ahab Repents

As soon as Jezebel gets the word she triumphantly tells her husband to "Get up and take possession of the vineyard of Naboth the Jezreelite that he refused to sell you. He is no longer alive, but dead." But Ahab's satisfaction will be short-lived, for when he gets to the vineyard, who should be waiting for him, but his old nemesis?

"You have sold yourself to do evil in the eyes of the Lord," shouts Elijah in fine form. I will bring disaster upon you and your descendants. "In the place where dogs licked up Naboth's blood, dogs will lick up your blood—yes, yours!" As for Jezebel, "Dogs will devour Jezebel by the wall of Jezreel."

And for the first time the prophet's words have an effect on the king. Either from terror at the gruesome picture Elijah conjures up, or genuine regret at his and Jezebel's misdeeds, or a little of both, Ahab tears his clothes off and puts on sackcloth. He fasts and becomes meek to demonstrate his newfound understanding. We do not hear of a similar change of attitude in Jezebel.

When God hears of Ahab's repentance, he is pleased and tells Elijah "Have you noticed how Ahab has humbled himself before me? Because he has humbled himself, I will not bring this disaster in his day, but I will bring it on his house in the days of his son." But why does God seek to punish Ahab's children for their father's crimes?

Elijah's Prophecies Come True

Ahab lives out his kingship in relative calm, but at his death Elijah's prophecies begin to come true. When the king is fatally wounded in battle, his chariot is taken to be cleansed of his blood. To dishonor Ahab's memory, God causes the chariot to be washed in a pool where prostitutes bathe. Afterwards, "the dogs lick up the blood, as the word of the Lord had declared."

The fate of Jezebel and their children are even worse. Her son Joram has become king of Israel. Since the Lord has promised that Ahab and Jezebel's children will suffer for the sins of their parents, he has an Israelite general Jehu anointed as king. This Jehu proves to be masterful at fulfilling the command to annihilate Ahab's family from Joram the king, to every one of Ahab's sons, relatives and friends. This includes the seventy sons and grandsons that Ahab had through his many wives and who are all beheaded at Jehu's command.

Jehu personally goes to Jezreel to take care of Jezebel herself. The queen has heard the news of her son's death and prepares to meet her executioner by carefully putting on makeup and arranging her hair. One can deplore the crimes the Bible charges her with, while still admiring Jezebel's chutzpah in fearlessly facing Jehu. "Have you come in peace, Zimri, you murderer of your master?" By calling him Zimri, the king who reigned for a mere seven days, Jezebel is taunting Jehu.

But the new king refuses to take the bait and ignoring the queen, simply orders his men to throw her out the window. "So they threw her down, and some of her blood spattered the wall and the horses as they trampled her underfoot." Jehu carefully waits until after he has dined before telling the servants to bury her. By then, nothing remains "except her skull, her feet and her hands." And they all remember Elijah's prophecy: "Jezreel dogs will devour Jezebel's flesh...so that no one will be able to say, 'This is Jezebel.'"

Jehu has carried out God's plan. Yet once he is established he too is "not careful to keep the law of the Lord, the God of Israel, with all his heart." In fact he is not much better than the man he killed and replaced, Ahab's son Joram. Although Joram also displeased God, the Bible tells us that "he was not as bad as his parents," and took down the pillars of Baal that his father had put up. So it is difficult to understand why he and his entire family had to die so that the not so good Jehu could take over.

A Chariot and Horses of Fire

Elijah lives to witness Ahab's death but not that of his family.

When the prophet realizes that the hour of his death is approaching, he urges his devoted friend and protégé to leave him. But Elisha is determined to stay with the man who is like a father to him to the end: "As surely as the Lord lives and as you live, I will not leave you." They are slowly walking toward the Jordan River, as a group of the Lord's prophets watch them. One says to Elisha, "Do you know that the Lord is going to take your master from you today?"

Elisha answers, "Yes, I know, but do not speak of it."

When the two reach the Jordan, the great prophet rolls up his cloak and strikes the water with it. Immediately the river "divides to the right and to the left, and the two of them cross over on dry ground." Facing Elisha, Elijah asks "what can I do for you before I am taken from you?"

Elisha fears that he will not be able to fill the great prophet's shoes, that he will be found wanting. So what he asks is to "Let me inherit a double portion of your spirit."

"You have asked a difficult thing," Elijah tells him, "yet if you see me when I am taken from you, it will be yours—otherwise not."

They are walking and talking together as they have always done, when suddenly before Elisha's eyes, appear a chariot with horses of fire. Then Elijah is snatched into the chariot and as Elisha cries out "My father! My father, the chariots and horsemen of Israel," the prophet is carried away to heaven in a whirlwind.

Elijah is gone forever, and the grief stricken Elisha takes hold of his clothes and tears them apart. But he must not allow himself to grieve too long for God's work awaits him. He picks up Elijah's cloak and as Elijah had done, strikes the water. And just as with Elijah, the river divides and Elisha crosses. The group of prophets is watching and they realize that "the spirit of Elijah is resting on Elisha." The mantle has been passed.

AMOS: REAL JUSTICE OVER RELIGIOUS RITUALS

> I despise your religious feasts; I cannot stand
> your assemblies.
> -Amos on what God really thinks (Amos 5:21)

"Get out, you seer! Go back to the land of Judah. Earn your bread there and do your prophesying there." Amaziah, priest to Jeroboam king of Israel lashed out at the simple shepherd before him. There was no reason for the powerful priest to fear this lone man. Yet he did, for he sensed that Amos was no ordinary troublemaker stirring up the people. Amaziah was right, for God spoke through Amos, a god that demanded justice and fairness.

The Lord had called this keeper of flocks to preach in the divided land of Israel and Judah in about 750 BC. He had seen in Amos a brave man, one unafraid to denounce corruption wherever he found it from the royal courts to the temple.

And so the shepherd began to speak out against all the abuses of power that he saw. To the dishonest merchants he railed how you "deal deceitfully with false balances." He promised God's wrath against those trading in slaves, who "buy the poor for silver and the needy for a pair of sandals."

No one had ever spoken of such things before. No one had ever declared God's rage against those who mistreat their fellowmen. The rulers of the land began to take notice of Amos as crowds gathered to listen. "I know how many are your offenses and how great your sins. You oppress the righteous and take bribes and you deprive the poor of justice in the courts." Who had ever cared before that judges could be bribed and did not judge fairly?

Most of all Amos denounced religious hypocrisy. You "bring your sacrifices every morning, your tithes every three years. You burn leavened bread as a thank offering and brag about your offerings." But do you think that God will excuse your evil conduct because of the rituals you practice? This is what the Lord thinks: "I despise your religious feasts; I cannot stand your assemblies. Even though you bring me burnt offerings and grain offerings, I will not accept them. Though you bring choice fellowship offerings, I will have no regard for them." What is empty ritual when you behave immorally?

As for the establishment priests, they were part and parcel of the corruption with their temple taxes. Scornfully Amos eyed Amaziah the powerful priest who had summoned him: "I am neither a prophet nor a prophet's son, but I am a shepherd, and a gatherer of sycamore fruit." Unlike you was the implication I do not make my living by taking money in the name of God. "But the Lord took me from tending the flock and said to me, 'Go, prophesy to my people Israel.'" Tell them what they need to know.

Amazingly, though he made no claims to magic or miracles, people listened to Amos. The miracle lay in the power of his words and it was this that would inspire those who came after him, including centuries later, another teacher called Jesus.

Listen said Amos, this is what the Lord wants you to know: "Away with the noise of your songs! I will not listen to the music of your harps. But let justice roll on like a river, and righteousness like a never-failing stream!"

HOSEA: A GOD WHO WANTS TO BE LOVED, NOT FEARED

> Go, take to yourself a whore and have children
> of whoredom.
> -God to Hosea (Hosea 1:2)

God Gives a Bizarre Order

The voice whispered to Hosea in his dream; the same voice he had heard the previous night and the night before that. Hosea knew in his heart that it was God speaking to him. Why the Lord would choose such a humble man as himself, Hosea could not fathom. But if God wanted Hosea to be his prophet than so be it; his devotion to God made him willingly accept his new role as God's spokesman. Willingly that is until in yet another dream God spoke such strange words that Hosea was dumbfounded. Go marry a prostitute the Lord ordered him! Have children by her. Was he mad? Were these truly the words of God?

Hosea Takes a Wife, God Rants about Infidelity

> For you are not my people and I am not your
> God. (Hosea 1:9)

In the next days, Hosea searches his mind and his heart, and at last begins to understand the Lord's thinking. At the same time he meets Gomer, the daughter of Diblaim. He had heard talk of her dissolute reputation. Yet the delicate looking young woman standing before him seemed troubled, not evil. Hosea and Gomer fall in love and Hosea's understanding is complete.

Hosea will marry a woman he truly loves and she will bear three children. Yet he will always have doubts about her and whether those children are his. Thus as a prophet, he will be able to speak with passionate certainty about a beloved spouse's infidelities, and accurately convey the anger and sadness that God himself is suffering. For that is how the Lord viewed his relationship with his people. They are worshipping other gods, abandoning the path of righteousness that the Lord has shown them, just like a wife who betrays her husband with other lovers.

Turning away from Violence and Terror: God Travels a New Road

At times, God whines and rants about punishment to Hosea. Nevertheless, he is quite different from the God of Joshua who killed indiscriminately and controlled the Israelites through terror. This god wants to be loved more than feared. And like an adolescent groping his way towards maturity, it has dawned on the Lord that fear and love are contradictory. He can force people to worship him with dread, to grovel and bow down to him. He can even compel his worshippers to pretend they love him. But of what use is that to him when it is all so meaningless? The Lord, after all, can see into their hearts to their true feelings. God comes to a startling revelation. Despite all his power, he can neither compel love nor morality. Love must be freely given and morality freely followed.

Hosea and God Divorce their Spouses

After years of marriage, Gomer leaves at Hosea's request. Whether Gomer has been truly unfaithful, her husband believes she has and his doubts have become unbearable to him. There follow long stretches of God complaining through Hosea about the Israelites and their betrayal. "And now they sin more and more, and make for themselves molten images." Like a rejected lover, he mourns, "I cared for you in the wilderness, in the land of drought."

God Reconciles with his People

Yet in the end there is reconciliation. God tells his prophet to once again "love a woman who is loved by her husband, yet an adulteress even as the Lord loves the sons of Israel, though they turn to other gods." Hosea goes out and buys a woman apparently for sale for "fifteen shekels of silver and a homer and a half of barley." There is no doubt that this woman is the wayward Gomer. Hosea brings her home and they are reconciled. No matter what she has done, Hosea loves her and will not let her go again.

As Hosea realizes his love for Gomer, so God recognizes his love for his people is much greater than his anger, and through his prophet, he speaks:

I will heal their apostasy,
I will love them freely,
For My anger has turned away from them.

God is evolving; he is on his way.

VI. EXILED TO THE EAST: BABYLONIA
(700-500 BC)

In 700 BC, the Northern Kingdom of Israel fell to the Assyrian Empire. According to the Bible, all of the inhabitants were deported and became known as "The Ten Lost Tribes." The Southern Kingdom of Judah fell a century later to Babylonia and many of the people were deported to Babylonian cities. The Book of Jeremiah reports the number as 4,600. This period is known as "The Exile."

When the Persians conquered Babylon in 539 BC, they allowed Jews to return to their former lands. Some opted to remain in their current homes, while others chose to return to what they hoped would be a rebuilding of the temple.

THE ANGEL RAPHAEL AS EXORCIST: TOBIAS
AND THE RESCUE OF SARA

When an innocent young woman is tormented by a devil, a young hero, and an angel exorcist are sent to the rescue. Add love, courage, and a tail-wagging dog and you have a most captivating and enchanting tale.

The Book of Tobit tells the story of two troubled families beginning with the goodhearted Tobit himself, a man devoted to his faith, his wife Anna, their son Tobias, and his people. Not an easy task for an exile living among hated conquerors in the Assyrian city of Nineveh. Tobit has already been punished for taking it upon himself to bury those of his rebellious countrymen killed by the authorities and denied decent burial.

An Evil Sleep

On a day that will bring much misfortune, Tobit has once again courageously buried a body. But this being a holy day, Tobit must sleep outside his house because he is temporarily unclean after touching the corpse. In a scene that is both comic and tragic, the sleeping Tobit is struck in the eyes by bird droppings. When he awakens, he is blind. This was, no doubt, an ancient explanation for the milky film of cataracts.

In the following days, with the sightless Tobit unable to work, the family's fortunes deteriorate to the point of poverty. Anna is forced to support the household with her spinning, which she does with much complaint. Feeling helpless and useless, Tobit becomes increasingly depressed to the point where he longs for death. "Now, O Lord, do with me according to thy will, and command my spirit to be received in peace: for it is better for me to die, than to live."

Sara, Possessed

In the far off city of Rages, there is another who wants to die. Sara, the only daughter of the wealthy Raguel and his wife—another Anna—has reached the desperation point. The young woman is the victim of a demon by the name of Asmodeus. How she came to be possessed is a mystery. But apparently this demon only attacks on her wedding night. Before the bride and groom can consummate their marriage, the apparently jealous Asmodeus murders the groom!

Seven times Sara has married, only to find herself almost immediately a widow. You would think that the men of the town would be a little wary of marriage with the afflicted young woman for they had surely all heard of these strange occurrences. But this is similar to a mythic story in which suitors vie for the hand of a princess by doing heroic deeds. Each of Sara's husbands thought that he would be the one to vanquish this devil and win the beautiful Sara along with her rich dowry.

Now to add to Sara's woes she has been accused by a malicious maidservant of herself being behind the deaths. So distraught does Sara become at this unjust accusation that she goes to an unused room of the house and for three days takes no food or drink. Her parents must be away, since they would surely have watched over her. But she is alone and like Tobit she wants to die. What does she have to live for she asks herself? But just when she has given up all hope, she prays to God: "To thee, O Lord, I turn my face; to thee I direct my eyes." She realizes how much her death would hurt her beloved parents, and slowly she finds a peace within herself "because after a storm thou makest a calm." Finally she gives up struggling to find the answers and puts her trust in God.

Tobias goes on a Quest

Meanwhile back in Ninevah, the unhappy Tobit hopes death will soon end his suffering. His only regret is leaving his wife and son to an uncertain future. How can he help them he agonizes? Suddenly he remembers a substantial loan he made many years ago to a close friend, Gabelus, now living in the city of Rages. Why not send Tobias to retrieve that loan. The youthful Tobias excitedly agrees. Not only will this ease his father's mind, but it will be a grand adventure. He even decides to take his beloved little dog with him. Only mother Anna is loath to let him go and despite her somewhat whiny nature, who can blame her. She knows her world is a very dangerous one. Will her only child ever return?

To calm Anna's fears and to help Tobias find his way, Tobit decides that a guide must be found and so Tobias goes into town to ask around. Suddenly he is approached by a man who introduces himself as Azarias. He claims to know the way to Rages very well, and offers his services. But who is this Azarias and why is he so eager to guide Tobias?

Unknown to all, God has been listening attentively to the prayers of two very troubled people. And this supposed guide is no less then the archangel Raphael come to earth in disguise to make things right for them. When Tobit meets his son's guide and hears his words, all anxiety vanishes. "I will lead thy son safe, and bring him to thee again safe."

As Anna bids a tearful farewell to her only child, Tobit anguishes that he has nothing of value to see his son off with. Except, he realizes, the wisdom of his faith and this he offers:

"See thou never do to another what thou wouldst hate to have done to thee by another."

"Seek counsel always of a wise man."

And, despite the difficulties with his wife:

"Thou shalt honor thy mother all the days of her life: For thou must be mindful what and how great perils she suffered for thee in her womb."

Tobias listens attentively and then embraces his father. With his new guide and his faithful dog, he is about to embark on a journey that will prove to be reminiscent of Homer's Odyssey, complete with monsters and the rescue of a beautiful maiden.

The youth faces his first challenge at the Tigris River. There a monstrous fish suddenly looms out of the water ready to do battle. Tobias is terrified, but at his side is Azarias encouraging him to "take him by the gill and draw him to thee." And despite his fright, Tobias bravely wrestles with the thrashing fish and taking him by the gill, pulls the beast onto the land where he kills him. Afterwards, the angel tells his young friend to do a strange thing: "Take out the entrails of this fish, and lay up his heart, and his gall, and his liver for thee: for these are necessary for useful medicines." How useful we will discover later.

The Angel Raphael Plays Matchmaker

Now that he has slain a monster, it is time for Tobias like any proper hero to rescue a maiden. He asks Azarias where they should stay for the night and the angel points to a house up ahead. There he says lives a man who happens to be a kinsman of yours who will show them hospitality. Within is also the man's good and beautiful daughter. Tobias he tells him, this is the woman who is destined to be your wife.

By now Tobias has realized that his guide is something more than a man and so he is inclined to believe what Azarias says. But when he hears the names Raguel and Sara, Tobias becomes wary. He has heard the story of Sara's seven dead husbands and has no desire to be the eighth! Trust me, Azarias urges, and I will tell you the secret of how to conquer a demon. For the first time, the younger man doubts his mentor, but keeps silent.

As they approach the doors, sitting within are Raguel and Anna and poor Sara. She is resigned to the fact that she will remain unmarried for the rest of her life. Never, she vows, will she put another man's life in danger. When two visitors seeking shelter for the night are announced by the servants, Sara pays little heed being too much involved in her own disturbing thoughts. But her father welcomes the travelers and immediately notes the resemblance to his brother Tobit. Where are you from he asks and when he hears it is Ninevah, "Do you know Tobit my brother?" And at Tobias' answer, Raguel goes to him "and kisses him with tears and weeping upon his neck."

"A blessing be upon thee, my son, because thou art the son of a good and most virtuous man." Then he presents his wife and there are more kisses and embraces. And then Sara comes forward, and all of Tobias' doubts are put to rest. Sara has a beauty and a sweetness of spirit that shine. And how does she feel about Tobias? She sees a handsome, smiling youth whose manner is more than pleasing to her. But she also knows that she must not go down that path ever again. She is doomed to be alone for the rest of her life.

Anna and Raguel are about to prepare a grand dinner for their new found relative, but now that he's made up his mind, Tobias is impatient "I will not eat nor drink here this day, unless thou first grant me my petition, and promise to give me Sara thy daughter." His only answer is silence. Sara and her parents are dazed, not so much at his hasty proposal, but because they assume that Tobias is unaware of Sara's sad marital history. Raguel finally warns his nephew that he fears for his life should he marry his daughter. But before he can continue, Tobias assures them that he knows everything and that he is confident he will win against Sara's demon.

Azarias too speaks: "Be not afraid to give her to this man, for to him who feareth God is thy daughter due to be his wife." Sara is afraid to hope but her father sees something in the angel's eyes that reassure him. "I doubt not but God hath regarded my prayers and tears in his sight." Then he takes Sara's hand and places it in the hand of Tobias, "may the God of Abraham, and the God of Isaac, and the God of Jacob be with you, and may he join you together, and fulfill his blessing in you."

"And taking paper they made a writing of the marriage." A ceremony isn't necessary, just a drawing up of papers. "And afterwards they made merry, blessing God." A bedchamber is prepared for the newly married couple and Anna weeps over her daughter fervently hoping that this time "the Lord of heaven will give thee joy for the trouble thou hast undergone."

The Devil Gets his Due (along with some fish liver)

Despite Tobias' brave words, Sara doubts that he will escape the fate of his predecessors, and she hesitates at entering the bedchamber. She must trust him her new husband bids her and all will be well. As she watches, Tobias takes "out of his bag part of the liver, and lays it upon the burning coals." Just then Sara begins to shake as she senses the approach of her persecutor, Asmodeus the demon, ready to once again wreak havoc on her wedding night. But this time a surprise lies awaiting the fiend. It turns out that the smell of burning fish liver is toxic to creatures such as him, and he collapses in a helpless, furious heap. Once Asmodeus is incapacitated, "the angel Raphael takes the devil, and binds him in the desert of upper Egypt."

Am I really free, Sara wonders? And is Tobias safe? Tobias smiles at her "Sara, arise, and let us pray to God to day, and to morrow, and the next day: because for these three nights we are joined to God: and when the third night is over, we will be in our own wedlock."

So for three nights the newlyweds do nothing but pray, while outside the anxious parents are hoping for the best but preparing for the worst. In fact, Raguel has had a grave dug just in case. On the fourth night Anna sends one of her servants to look in on them and "finds them safe and sound, sleeping both together." Weeping happily, Raguel and Anna bless the Lord, "for thou hast shown thy mercy to us, and hast shut out from us the enemy that persecuted us."

Now that he and Sara are safely married, Tobias is anxious to return home "for thou knowest that my father numbereth the days: and if I stay one day more, his soul will be afflicted." One last task remains: to retrieve the loan from Tobit's friend Gabelus. After all, wasn't this the reason for Tobias' journey in the first place? Gabelus is found, gratefully returns the loan and even attends the wedding feast.

Tobias is now a rich man, for as well as the returned loan, Raguel has already given him half his property. He cannot wait to see his parents and tell them all the amazing adventures he has had and most of all present their new daughter-in-law to them. And with tears of both sadness and joy, Raguel and Anna wish a safe journey to their daughter and son-in-law.

A Son Returns, a Father is Miraculously Healed

It is none too soon, for Tobias has been away long enough and his mother has been making his father's life even more hellish, adding guilt to his misery. Didn't he push Tobias to go, she continually berates him? If their only son should fail to return, it will be his fault. In spite of her meanness, one can still feel sympathy for Anna as day after day she faithfully climbs the hill where she can watch for that first glimpse of her child. Will this finally be the hour of his return, she asks herself each day?

The grieving couple has just about given up hope when in the distance Anna catches sight of two men and a dog. She holds her breath, and as the little group draws near, it is clear that her son has come home. They are alone for Azarias had suggested they go on ahead quickly and leave Sara and the animals to travel at a more leisurely pace, since Tobias is so concerned about his parents.

Anna runs to tell her trembling husband who "rising up, began to run stumbling with his feet, and giving a servant his hand, went to meet his son. And receiving him kissed him, as did also his wife, and they began to weep for joy." Not to be outdone, "the dog, which had been with them in the way, ran before, and coming as if he had brought the news, showed his joy by his fawning and wagging his tail."

After they had all given thanks to God, Tobias tells his father to have patience with what he is about to do and not be afraid. Taking the gall of the fish, he lays it upon his father's eyes just as Azarias has instructed. For one half hour they wait, and then "a white skin began to come out of his eyes, like the skin of an egg. And Tobit took hold of it, and drew it from his eyes, and recovered his sight."

Tobit looks upon Tobias and is overwhelmed at the wonder. "I bless thee, O Lord God of Israel, because thou hast chastised me, and thou hast saved me and behold I see Tobias my son." When his new daughter-in-law arrives a week later, he is able to see her as well. "For seven days they feast and rejoice all with great joy."

There is only one thing that disturbs them: how to properly repay the man who has done so much for them. Tobias recounts how he would have been devoured by a monster fish if not for Azarias. Then of course there is Sara. "He caused me to have my wife, and he chased from her the evil spirit." And he brought me safely home and allowed my father to look upon his son. "What can we give him sufficient for these things?"

Father and son finally agree to give their benefactor half of all their new wealth and call him in. When he hears their intention, Azarias gently laughs, and reveals his true identity. "I am the angel Raphael, one of the seven who stand before the Lord." At his words they fall upon the ground in fright, but he quickly tells them "Peace be unto you, fear not."

"The Lord sent me to heal thee, and to deliver Sara thy son's wife from the devil." Now it is time for him to return to the Lord. "And when he had said these things, he was taken from their sight, and they could see him no more." He was gone leaving a most happy family behind.

Note: The Book of Tobit has had a somewhat rocky history. It was included in the Septuagint, the Greek translation of the Hebrew Scriptures for Jews in the third century BC, who had become less than fluent in Hebrew. But it was excluded from later Bibles by Jewish scholars. Catholic Bibles put it in, while some Protestant versions have it and some don't. This is a shame, because with its delightful blend of magical doings with very real human emotions, frailties and strengths, it deserves more attention. Along with its strong and loving family bonds, not to mention a happy tail-wagging dog, it is a delightful tale.

DANIEL FOR THE DEFENSE: THE TRIAL OF SUSANNA

Now Susanna was a very delicate woman, and
beauteous to behold."
-Book of Susanna 1:31

The Accused

When a woman is accused of wrongdoing by two malicious judges, God inspires a devout young man to use reason to prove her innocence and save her life.

The time is the Babylonian exile in 600 BC. A large group of Jews has gathered to hear the sensational case of a young wife accused of adultery, an act punishable by death! There are those in the crowd who relish the spectacle of this beautiful, wealthy woman brought low, and enjoy hearing all the salacious details. Self-righteously they justify their satisfaction by telling each other that she deserves to pay the ultimate price. Surely it is an open and shut case; the accusers are two of the most esteemed judges in the community, while the defendant is a mere woman whose beauty in itself is surely confirmation of her guilt.

But there is one in the gathering who has grave doubts, and he is not the kind to remain silent. He is Daniel, a man devoted to God and to truth. A keen judge of character, Daniel can detect no sign of falsehood in Susanna, while every gesture and expression of her accusers screams liar.

Unaware of her supporter, Susanna has given up hope. Even more than for herself, Susanna grieves for her family who have stood by her, the righteous parents who had always "taught their daughter according to the law of Moses," her good husband Joacim to whom "resorted the Jews; because he was more honorable than all others." Most of all there are her children who will not only lose their mother, but be branded the children of an adulteress.

Susanna had tried to tell the real story but no one in authority would listen. Their leaders had become lazy and unwilling to challenge one of their own. Moreover, those in the crowd calling for her execution were loud and demanding. Why not give them what they wanted.

When she hears the verdict—death—Susanna cries out to God "Thou knowest that they have borne false witness against me, and, behold, I must die; whereas I never did such things as these men have maliciously invented against me." Daniel is struck by her words, more than ever convinced of her innocence, and sure that the Lord is urging him to save her.

The Accusers

> The assembly believed them as they were the
> elders and judges of the people: so they
> condemned her to death.
> -Book of Susanna 1:41

There are two others in the assembly who know the truth and they listen to the decree with smug approval. These two respected judges or elders think back to the day when this insolent young woman denied their attentions. How dared she? She had enthralled both of them with her beauty and they had taken every opportunity to go to the house of Joacim and feast their eyes on his wife. No one suspected their motives for they were influential leaders in Babylon's Jewish community. Nor were they aware of each other's evil intentions, until one day "they parted the one from the other, and turning back again they came to the same place; after that they had asked one another the cause, and acknowledged their lust."

Thus, the two learn they are kindred spirits and plot how they will force themselves on Susanna. This isn't the first time that each had abused a woman, but their position is such that none had dared complain.

Now Susanna was the intended victim. Unknown to her, she was being closely observed and one day the two hid themselves while she was bathing, and watched her. The garden doors were locked and Susanna alone when her would-be rapists reveal themselves. Susanna was shocked when they threatened to tell everyone she had a lover unless she submitted to their demands. No one including your husband will ever know, they tell her, so why not just do as we ask. If you try to incriminate us, no one will believe you.

Susanna soon realizes how diabolically complete the trap is. But unlike other women in the community who feared these men too much to disobey, Susanna refuses to give in. Better to risk these wicked ones telling their lies, she thinks, then to do wrong in her own eyes as well as "sin in the sight of the Lord." Quickly the innocent woman cries out, but the judges, enraged at her refusal are quicker and louder as they rush to open the garden door. With the whole household converging on the garden, the elders declare that Susanna had had a man with her. They command that she be tried before the Jewish community uncaring that she will die if found guilty.

The story the elders tell is full of holes, but because of their influence and standing in the community, it is automatically accepted. "And when we saw them together, the man we could not hold: for he was stronger than we, and opened the door, and leaped out." No one dares to question the judges and a verdict is quickly reached.

The Defender

Thou hast pronounced false judgment and hast
condemned the innocent and hast let the guilty
go free.
-Book of Susanna 1:53

As Susanna is being led away to die, disturbing words suddenly ring out; 'I will not have this innocent woman's blood upon my conscience.' The mob halts in confusion, and turns to the man whose intensity of manner and speech command their attention. "What mean these words that thou hast spoken?"

Looking out with piercing eyes over all, Daniel is eloquent, and the senseless crowd, so ready to kill, pays attention: "Are ye such fools, ye sons of Israel, that without examination or knowledge of the truth ye have condemned a daughter of Israel?" You must "return again to the place of judgment" and discover who has truly told the facts and who has lied. Even the leaders of the community are impressed, "come, sit down among us, and show it us, seeing God hath given thee the honor of an elder."

Daniel's method is simple and effective; he will separate the accusers. "Put these two aside one far from another, and I will examine them." The elders protest, but they no longer have the people in their pockets and Daniel soon has his way. The first judge is brought forward, while the second is taken far away where he cannot hear. No longer arrogant, the elder is struggling to hide his fear as the stern-faced Daniel pins him with a glare. You claim you saw Susanna and her lover together. "Now then, if thou hast seen her, tell me, under what tree sawest thou them companying together?"

The elder hesitates; then replies "Under a mastick tree." Daniel has him taken away and the second elder brought in. He too trembles when the same question is put to him. "Now therefore tell me, under what tree didst thou take them companying together? "Under an holm tree," is his answer.

Judgment

> From that day forth was Daniel had in great
> reputation in the sight of the people.
> -Book of Susanna 1:64

There is a hush over the people. The truth stands starkly as Daniel's voice rings out "O thou that art waxen old in wickedness, now thy sins which thou hast committed aforetime are come to light."

Their terror equal to their wickedness, the elders shake at Daniel's wrath. "The angel of God waiteth with the sword to cut thee in two, that he may destroy you."

The thoughtless crowd, so ready to execute an innocent woman, has finally, rightfully turned against the guilty. "All the assembly cried out with a loud voice...And they arose against the two elders, for Daniel had convicted them of false witness by their own mouth."

"And according to the law of Moses they did unto them in such sort as they maliciously intended to do to their neighbor: and they put them to death. Thus the innocent blood was saved the same day."

Susanna is disbelieving. In a short space of time, she has traveled from condemned woman to innocence and freedom. She and her husband, parents and children weep for joy. They had always believed in her innocence and now "Chelcias and his wife praise God for their daughter Susanna, with Joacim her husband, and all the kindred, because there was no dishonesty found in her."

The story of Susanna and Daniel is one of great courage and conscience. How one woman bravely defies two influential, immoral men and one youth stands up to weak-minded, careless leaders and a senseless mob make this a powerfully inspiring tale.

HEROINES OF THE HAREM: VASHTI THE ARAB AND ESTHER THE JEW

> Later when the anger of King Xerxes had
> subsided, he remembered Vashti and what she
> had done and what he had decreed about her.
> -Esther 2:1

There are two women of courage in the Book of Esther: one is the title character, and the second is her Arab predecessor, Queen Vashti. They are both the wives of Xerxes the Persian King. This fascinating story, with its talk of harems, Arabian perfumes, and concubines, often resembles more the Tales of the Arabian Nights than it does the stark tales of Genesis or Exodus.

The King and the Persian Court

Vashti to the King: "No," to Displaying Herself at a Drunken Party!

The saga begins with King Xerxes of Persia giving a sumptuous banquet lasting for seven days. All of the greatest nobles, military leaders and princes in his vast empire are in attendance. With wine flowing freely, the men are having a pretty wild time of it, and on the seventh day, the king decides to send for his wife, Queen Vashti, "so he can display her beauty" to all his men. Even on the surface, this sounds bad enough, but there is some suggestion that he wanted her to appear naked, with just her royal crown on, and nothing else! He has after all displayed all of his other marvelous possessions and now it is time to show off his prize piece.

Now Vashti is hosting her own feast for the wives, when she gets the message that Xerxes wants her to parade around in front of a bunch of drunken louts. The other women watch closely for the Queen's reaction. The envious ones take a vicious pleasure at her prospective humiliation, while others who must also cope with tyrannical spouses are sympathetic. What is Vashti to do? As a woman, she must obey her husband. Moreover this husband is also a ruler constantly in need of impressing his subjects with his power and authority.

Why would a husband even think of displaying his wife in so degrading a fashion? Was it merely his intoxication speaking? Has he sought to shame her before this? Perhaps Vashti has been a defiant wife and there have been arguments between them. She is after all a proud princess herself from a royal house. She may not have been as subservient as her temperamental spouse wished and now he seeks to punish her for her arrogance.

If she refuses to go, the consequences may be dire. Yet Vashti informs the messenger that she is not coming. Upon hearing those words, the king explodes. Not only has Vashti defied him but she has done so in front of all of his guests. His advisers egg him on by pointing out how all of the noble ladies have witnessed the queen's insolent conduct. If the king doesn't act quickly, news of Vashti's disobedience will spread throughout the land like an infection, inciting all women to act independently and defiantly.

In his angry, drunken state, Xerxes needs no more prodding. Declaring "that every man should be ruler over his own household," he decrees that Vashti is no longer queen and is never to come into his presence again. Is Vashti shocked? Certainly she had known the risk she was taking and she is lucky to escape with her life. But she had decided that her dignity and sense of self were more important than anything else, including being queen. Then too maybe she had had her fill of this tyrant. Where Vashti goes after her banishment and what happens to her, we do not know.

Vashti has often gotten a bad press. In Talmudic writings, for instance, she is seen as a cruel taskmaster, one who deserves her punishment. But it should be noted that she was identified as the descendant of one of the most hated conquerors of the Israelites, King Nebuchadnezzar of Babylon, destroyer of the great Temple. As a member of that house, she was unlikely to garner much sympathy among these chroniclers.

Does Xerxes ever regret his foolish, inebriated command? Does he ever miss Vashti? If he does, even he cannot undo a royal edict.

The Jewess Esther Wins a Persian Beauty Contest

After a few years of loneliness, the king decides he needs another wife and orders his officials to organize a countrywide beauty contest. "Let a search be made for beautiful young virgins." And this time there will be no more proud princesses, only meek subjects need apply.

Now in the Persian city of Susa, there lives a Jewish exile by the name of Mordecai. Living with him is his young cousin and ward Esther. Why not bring the lovely Esther to the attention of the king's commissioners in hopes that she will win the king's favor, thinks Mordecai. Just what is he thinking of? He surely understands that if his plans are successful, his cousin will in affect be part of a foreign harem even if she is the queen. Can it be that Mordecai foresees a time when the Jews will need a strong influence at court and is willing in a sense to sacrifice his beloved, adopted daughter?

And what does Esther think; does she unquestioningly go along with Mordecai's wishes? Surely she is afraid—everyone has heard of the way the king treated Vashti. And what about having to lie about her Jewish identity since Mordecai fears that it will jeopardize her chances of becoming queen? But she loves Mordecai, who has cared for her since she was orphaned as a small child. All of her life she has obediently listened to him and trusts him to know what is right.

Yet undeniably another thought is going through her mind. What about the dazzling possibility that she Esther could become queen of the great empire of Persia? She would live in a glorious palace; have the most beautiful clothes, and endless servants to do her bidding. It's a heady prospect for a modest girl living a simple life.

Through her beauty and grace, Esther becomes a finalist in this "Miss Persia" competition and along with her rivals is brought to the palace harem. For the next twelve months all of the women undergo a rigorous training program in how to please the king. And after six months of beauty treatments with oil of myrrh, perfumes and cosmetics, Esther is ready to charm the Persian monarch.

Esther knows the rules. "In the evening she will go there and in the morning return to another part of the harem to the care of Shaashgaz, the king's eunuch who is in charge of the concubines. She will not return to the king unless he is pleased with her and summons her by name."

As it turns out, the king is very pleased with the lovely, amiable and compliant Esther. "And she won his favor and approval more than any of the other virgins. So he set a royal crown on her head and made her queen." Happily Xerxes proclaims a holiday and gives a banquet in his new wife's honor.

And Esther—is she happy? She has dutifully complied with Mordecai's wishes, and with her sweet temperament, has won the heart of the volatile king. But at what price? She cannot now freely see her beloved foster father because he is known to be a Jew and that would bring suspicion on her. Does she also have to worship foreign gods? Xerxes is a Zoroastrian* and Esther may have to pretend to be a believer as well.

*Note: Zoroastrianism was the religion of Persia. It is sometimes called a dual religion or a precursor to monotheism and Christianity as well. Its main figure is the god of light and good, Ahura Mazda and opposing him is a god of darkness. Because the two forces are considered equal, it is more dualistic than monotheistic. But like Judaism, Zoroastrianism was very different from the usual faiths of the time with their multitudes of gods.

Still, Esther tells herself she is a lucky woman. Her husband adores her and she has all the material things a woman could wish for. If she ever thinks of Vashti and how precarious a queen's position is, she determines that unlike her predecessor, she will never give her husband any reason to dislike her and put her away.

Does Mordecai miss Esther now that his plan has been such a success? He still worries about her and always sits at the king's gate should his foster daughter ever need him. One day he happens to overhear two officers plotting to assassinate the king! Immediately he sends a message to Esther, who swiftly warns Xerxes, giving credit to Mordecai without revealing their relationship. The plotters are duly executed and the whole affair is written up in the king's report book.

Enter the Villain: Court Counselor Haman

Now the king appoints an evil man, Haman, as his chief minister. Everyone from high nobles to the lowest subjects prudently pay homage and bow down to this highest official, all that is except one man. Each day when the new minister goes in through the king's gate, there sits Mordecai, rigidly unbent of knee and unbowed of head.

Why does Mordecai act so provocatively and thus call attention to himself? Haman is an Amalekite and there is a long history of bad blood between the Jews and the Amalakites. Is Mordecai being needlessly stubborn and inflammatory? It is after all just a simple bow. Or has Haman already tried to injure the Jewish population?

Haman is livid at Mordecai's behavior. That anyone should dare not give him his due is unforgivable, least of all some simpleton of a Jew! But wily Haman ponders how he can get revenge not just on Mordecai but on the entire Jewish community of Persia.

Minister Haman goes to the king and slyly tells him of a certain people scattered throughout his empire "whose customs are different from those of all other people and who do not obey the king's laws; it is not in the king's best interest to tolerate them." If the king will give Haman free license to deal with them, all will be well.

Most probably Xerxes was neither for nor against the Jews, but carelessly paid little attention to what Haman said. If there were people in his empire who did not obey his laws, then let Haman do as he pleased, the king had other matters to contend with. The evil minister loses no time, issuing edicts in the king's name "to destroy, kill and annihilate all the Jews-young and old, women and little children-on a single day, the thirteenth day of the twelfth month, the month of Adar, and to plunder their goods."

When Mordecai hears the terrible news, he starts wailing bitterly, then tears his clothes, and dons sackcloth and ashes. Esther who as yet knows nothing about the edicts hears of Mordecai's strange behavior and sends her servant to find out what is wrong. She soon learns the grave danger the Jews face in every province. And according to Mordecai, it is Esther who must save them. She must go to the king and beg him to spare her people.

Esther is stunned. She will do all she can, but what Mordecai asks is impossible. For anyone, including the queen, to go into the king's presence in his inner court without first being summoned means death. There is but one exception: should the king extend his golden scepter to the offender, his or her life will be spared. But there is something else that Mordecai must be aware of. It has been a month since the king sent for her. Xerxes may be tired of her. He may be interested in another woman or women. Esther tells her cousin she is helpless.

Mordecai had rarely reprimanded his gentle, respectful ward, but now he is angered by her reluctance to involve herself and sternly warns "Do not think that because you are in the king's house you alone of all the Jews will escape." If you remain silent "you and your father's family will perish."

Queen Esther Takes Command

Throughout her life Esther has been meek and obedient. Passively she has accepted what others have ordained for her. Now she may feel a bit resentful at Mordecai for putting her in this position. It was he who made her queen and it was he who refused to bow down to Haman. Why should she suffer for his actions? But Esther quickly realizes that Haman would have used any excuse to hurt her people. And perhaps Mordecai is right in thinking that God made her queen for just this role. Somehow she must find the strength of mind and purpose to save her people and herself.

She thinks of that other woman, that other queen who once occupied her place. The strong minded Vashti was willing to do what she felt was right no matter the consequences. She, Esther, will also do what is right. And if she should die for it, then so be it.

With a new inner strength, Esther devises a plan. First she sends a message to her cousin to "gather together all the Jews who are in Susa, and fast for me. Do not eat or drink for three days, night or day. I and my maids will fast as you do. When this is done, I will go to the king, even though it is against the law. And if I perish, I perish." Now it is Mordecai who obeys Esther and does all she asks.

On the third day Esther puts on her most lavish robes and has her maids carefully arrange her hair. At peace with her decision, she goes to the entrance of the king's hall and calmly waits to see what the king will do. Xerxes sees the queen and is astonished. A myriad of thoughts occupy his mind. What is she doing here? She knows it is against the law—that it means death. And then, how beautiful she looks and how long since he's seen her. He smiles. Quickly he holds out to her the gold scepter and Esther approaches. "What is it, Queen Esther? What is your request? Even up to half the kingdom, it will be given you."

"If it pleases the king," Esther replies, "let the king, together with Haman, come today to a banquet I have prepared for him." The king is intrigued by this new, less timid wife. "Bring Haman at once," the king said, "so that we may do what Esther asks."

So the king and his minister go to the dinner that Esther has prepared. As they relax over the wine, the king once again asks his wife "Now what is your petition? It will be given you."

Demurely the queen answers "My petition and my request is this: If the king regards me with favor and if it pleases the king to grant my petition and fulfill my request, let the king and Haman come tomorrow to the banquet I will prepare for them. Then I will answer the king's question."

Having dined alone with the royal couple, Haman is in high spirits. Then he sees his challenger at the gate. Once again Mordecai fails to honor him and Haman is filled with rage. He complains to his wife and friends that all his great good fortune is as nothing because of "that Jew Mordecai sitting at the king's gate." And they suggest a solution that delights Haman. "Have a gallows built, seventy-five feet high, and ask the king tomorrow to have Mordecai hanged on it. Then go with the king to the dinner and be happy."

That night the king suffers from insomnia and to pass the time has his record book read to him. He listens to the account of how Mordecai saved his life and discovers that his rescuer has received no reward. The king considers himself a generous man and is stricken at this lack. Now it so happens that Haman is at this moment arriving to speak to the king about hanging Mordecai on the gallows he has just built.

Xerxes has his advisor immediately brought in. "What should be done for the man the king delights to honor," the king asks. And the vain minister thinks of course that it is he Haman who the king wants to honor. So he tells the king, "For the man the king delights to honor, have them bring a royal robe the king has worn and a horse the king has ridden, one with a royal crest placed on its head. Then let the robe and horse be entrusted to one of the king's most noble princes. Let them robe the man the king delights to honor, and lead him on the horse through the city streets, proclaiming before him, 'This is what is done for the man the king delights to honor!'"

"Go at once," the king commands Haman. "Get the robe and the horse and do just as you have suggested for Mordecai the Jew, who sits at the king's gate. Do not neglect anything you have recommended."

What! Mordecai the Jew? Caught in his own trap, Haman can do nothing but smile in agreement. He gets the robe and the horse, puts the robe on Mordecai and leads him on horseback through the streets, and, though he almost chokes, proclaims to the crowds, "This is what is done for the man the king delights to honor!" Afterwards Mordecai returns to the king's gate and Haman rushes home in a state.

The minister is grumbling to his wife and friends when the king's men come to escort him to Esther's second banquet. All three are drinking wine when the king once again asks, "Queen Esther, what is your petition? It will be given you. What is your request? Even up to half the kingdom, it will be granted." This time Esther gives him an answer: "If I have found favor with you, O king, and if it pleases your majesty, grant me my life-this is my petition. And spare my people-this is my request. For I and my people have been sold for destruction and slaughter and annihilation."

The king is appalled at her words. "Who is he? Where is the man who has dared to do such a thing?" Esther stands tall and points to the now quivering Haman "The adversary and enemy is this vile Haman." And she relates Haman's malignant intentions.

So sickened is the king at the revelation of his trusted minister's true nature that he quickly escapes to the palace garden for some air. As he is leaving, Haman reads his fate in the king's eyes, and desperately starts to plead for his life with the queen. But nothing is going right for the errant minister. The king is returning just as Haman is falling on the couch where Esther is sitting. He is outraged, mistakenly assuming that Haman is about to attack Esther. "Will he even molest the queen while she is with me in the house?"

At a signal, palace guards rush in to drag Haman away. But while the now ex-counselor is still within hearing, Harbona, one of the chamberlains obligingly notes, "A gallows seventy-five feet high stands by Haman's house. He had it made for Mordecai, who spoke up to help the king."

The still smoldering king bellows "Hang him on it!"

So Haman was executed—ironically—on the very device he had erected for Mordecai. However, not even the king can revoke the destructive edicts issued against the Jews in his name. He must issue new edicts giving them the right to unite and arm themselves against those who seek to harm them. Thus a day that was to be one of sorrow for the Jews turns into one of celebration as they fight their foes and win victory.

Over 75,000 of the enemy are slaughtered. Yet it is here at the end of the story that the Book of Esther turns rather dark and bloodthirsty with its emphasis on vengeance. The king's orders give the Jews not only the right "to destroy, kill and annihilate any armed force of any nationality or province that might attack them," but also their women and children. Esther herself begs the king to execute Haman's ten sons. Are they all as evil as their father? Or did it not matter how evil they were in a world in which a son paying for the crimes of the father is perfectly acceptable?

Yet the prophet Ezekiel (622-570 BC) had stressed that God did not want children to be punished for the sins of their parents. "Good people will be rewarded for doing good, and evil people will suffer for the evil they do. A son is not to suffer because of his father's sins."*

Despite the distracting focus on violent detail at the end, one remembers the true heart of the tale: that of two women who never meet, yet nevertheless share a bond. When Esther must find the courage to save her people, it is Vashti's brave example that inspires her to find it within herself.

*Ezekiel 18:19-20

VII. DOES GOD EVOLVE?

The God of Abraham, the God of Joshua, the God of Amos and Jonah. They are not the same. God changes and so do his people. Sometimes his people—as when Abraham lectures God about ethics regarding Sodom and Gomorrah—are more advanced than he is; at others, God has to drag reluctant humans into the light.

JONAH: A KINDER, GENTLER GOD PREACHES TOLERANCE TO A BACKWARD PROPHET

> You hurled me into the deep, into the very heart
> of the seas, and the currents swirled about me.
> -Jonah 2:3

Take a kinder, gentler god and a defiant, bloodthirsty prophet, and you get the story of Jonah.

Gimme That Old-Time Religion and a God of Violence

Jonah's troubles begin when God tells him to go preach in the city of Ninevah, the great capital city of the flowering civilization of Assyria, to the north of Palestine. God is much concerned about the Ninevites, for their ways have turned wicked. He will send his most persuasive prophet to get them on track. But Jonah balks. Why should he care about the Ninevites or their problems when they are, after all, Israel's past enemy, her cruel conqueror? He is content to preach and teach to his own people and no one else. If the Ninevites are bad then God should destroy them without anymore fuss as he did Sodom and Gomorrah.

Jonah's resentment at what he considers God's misplaced concern builds and instead of going to Ninevah, he runs away. Heading for the seacoast town of Joppa, he finds a ship bound for the Spanish city of Tarshish, which to Jonah's mind is at the ends of the earth. There the rebellious prophet foolishly believes he can escape God's notice.

Throw me Overboard

Then the Lord sent a great wind on the sea, and such a violent storm arose that the ship threatened to break up. -Jonah 1:4

After paying his fare, Jonah goes below and falling into a deep sleep is unaware of the howling winds and pelting rain suddenly assailing the vessel. The crew is filled with terror that the violent storm will sink the ship. Desperately they throw all the cargo overboard to lighten the ship's load, and each man cries out to his own particular god to save them.

The captain, remembering his passenger, goes below to rouse him. Shaking Jonah from the depths of slumber, the anxious captain shouts "how can you sleep? Get up and call upon your god! Maybe he will take notice of us, and we will not perish."

At once Jonah understands the reason for the storm. When the seamen draw lots to see who is responsible for their plight, the wayward prophet is unsurprised when the lot falls on him. All stare at the stranger and demand to know what he has done and what god "is responsible for making all this trouble for us? What is your country? From what people are you?"

A contrite Jonah replies that he is a Jew who worships the Lord. "I know that it is my fault that this great storm has come upon you." He has no desire to be the cause of their deaths and urges them to "pick me up and throw me into the sea, and it will become calm."

The men are at a loss. They are good people who neither want to offend Jonah's god, who has earned their trembling respect, nor hurt Jonah. The sailors attempt to row back to land, but the winds gust with growing intensity, battering the ship against the heaving waves. What is the right thing to do, they agonize, as Jonah continues to insist they throw him into the sea. "O Lord," they cry "please do not let us die for taking this man's life. Do not hold us accountable for killing an innocent man, for you, O Lord, have done as you pleased."

At last and with his consent, "they take Jonah and throw him overboard, and the raging sea grows calm." The awestruck sailors thank the Lord and make vows to him.

A Fishy Miracle

Now Jonah is adrift in the raging waters and not wanting him to die, God sends a huge fish to the rescue. The fish does the only thing he can do and swallows Jonah. Could this alleged fish really have been a whale? It is certainly true that people at the time would not have known the difference between a seagoing mammal and a fish. Moreover the animal had to be big enough to swallow a grown man. So maybe it was a whale. Whatever it was, Jonah is now residing in its belly.

It must have been dark, dank and smelly in this fish's innards. Nevertheless, an appreciative Jonah is ecstatic to be alive and offers up prayers of thanksgiving. After three days of praying in the fish's belly, God decides that both Jonah and the fish have had enough and he directs the fish to spew Jonah out onto dry land.

Jonah and the Vine

No doubt Jonah was hoping that God has forgotten their original disagreement. No such luck. Once again God commands Jonah to go to Ninevah, and this time Jonah is wise enough to obey, even if his heart isn't in the project. Yet even a reluctant Jonah is inspiring, and the Ninevites, from the greatest to the smallest, are moved to change their ways. The king himself declares "let everyone call urgently on God. Let them give up their evil ways and their violence."

"When God saw their willingness to reform, he was glad and did not bring upon them the destruction he had threatened." Does this satisfy Jonah? Not at all—Jonah wants the return of the wrathful god of the good old days. And he rails at the Lord, "This is why I was so quick to flee to Tarshish. I knew that you are a gracious and compassionate God, slow to anger and abounding in love, a God who relents from sending calamity."

Why is Jonah so stubborn? To be fair, Jonah is not used to the path that God is now following. He is accustomed to the angry deity who destroyed almost the entire earth in a flood, and the vengeful god of Joshua who cleansed Canaan of every man, woman, child and beast. Jonah cannot accept a god of compassion who reaches out to all peoples. So disgusted is Jonah that uncaring, he tells God to "take away my life, for it is better for me to die than to live." Then he goes outside the city to sit and sulk, still hoping that God will get tough on Ninevah.

But God cares about Jonah and wants him to understand. Since it is hot and uncomfortable where Jonah sits, God creates a vine and "makes it grow up over Jonah to give shade for his head to ease his discomfort, and Jonah is very happy about the vine." But then God sends a worm to chew the vine so it withers. And when the sun rises, God produces a blazing sun and a scorching wind. Jonah is not happy about this. In fact he grows faint and says "It would be better for me to die than to live."

Patiently the Lord says to Jonah. "Do you have a right to be angry about the vine?" Jonah insists he does. "I am angry enough to die." Then the Lord points out that Jonah has been concerned about the vine "though you did not tend it or make it grow. It sprang up overnight and died overnight. But Nineveh has more than a hundred and twenty thousand people." And God continues, "Should I not be concerned about that great city?"

Does Jonah understand at last?

RUTH VS. EZRA: ON NOT MISTREATING FOREIGN WIVES

> Let us make a covenant with our God to send
> away all the foreign wives as well as their
> children.
> -Ezra 10:3

One of the most exemplary women in the Bible is Ruth. Yet had the later prophet Ezra been around he would have told her husband to abandon her and their children, for despite her loyal and loving nature and her acceptance of God, Ruth had been born a Moabitess, a foreign woman.

An Alien Daughter-in-Law's Devotion

Like many a Bible story, the book of Ruth begins with a famine in the land in about 1000 BC. To find relief, Elimelech, his wife Naomi and two sons Mahlon and Chilion leave their stricken town of Bethlehem for Moab. There they settle down and in time Mahlon and Chilion take two Moabite

169

women as wives, Ruth and Orpah. Interestingly, there is no comment here, negative or otherwise, about the men marrying Gentile women. The family is content until a series of calamities befall them. First Elimelech dies, then in quick succession the two sons.

With her family gone, Naomi starts longing for her people back home and makes plans to return. She encourages her daughters-in-law to go back to their families, and to eventually remarry. "Go, return each of you to her mother's house. May the Lord deal kindly with you as you have dealt with the dead and with me."

At first both women insist they will go with her. But Naomi persists and eventually Orpah embraces her mother-in-law and leaves. Ruth, however, adamantly refuses to go. A great bond has developed between her and Naomi and they are like mother and daughter. Ruth is well aware of how desolate and alone her mother-in-law feels, hide it though she might. Ruth turns to the older woman and here speaks the words that have resonated through the centuries.

"Do not urge me to leave you or turn back from following you; for where you go, I will go, and where you lodge, I will lodge. Your people shall be my people, and your God, my God. Where you die, I will die, and there I will be buried."

This is what Naomi has been hoping to hear, but she wanted it to come from Ruth without any prompting. She loves the girl too much to ask her to leave all that is familiar to her for new hardships and an unknown land unless it is what Ruth truly wants to do. But although Ruth may be gentle, she is not without a sense of adventure and to leave this place of sorrow and start fresh somewhere else is appealing.

Ruth says goodbye to her family and the two women begin their journey back to Naomi's hometown, a difficult trip for two lone women, but at last they arrive in Bethlehem. For Naomi it is a bittersweet homecoming reminding her of all she has lost. Still she knows she is lucky to have Ruth with her. "Is this Naomi," all who see her exclaim in welcome. Naomi relates all that has happened to her and presents Ruth as the daughter-in-law who left her own home to come with her. Some look askance at this foreign woman, others nod approvingly at the look of affection and respect she shows Naomi.

Romance in the Barley Fields

The two women settle into Naomi's old house with Ruth finding ways to support them. It is barley harvesting time, and with Naomi's consent Ruth goes into the fields to pick up any remaining grain. The field she chooses happens to be owned by the prosperous farmer Boaz, a relative of Naomi's late husband. On that day, Boaz has come into the field to check on the harvesting and is struck by the sight of the lovely young woman hard at work.

Who is she, he asks one of his servants and on being told her identity, he approaches Ruth and introduces himself. Ruth is amazed when Boaz tells her she can stay in his fields and find all the grain that she needs. "Indeed, I have commanded the servants not to touch you. When you are thirsty, go to the water jars and drink from what the servants draw."

Overwhelmed with his generosity, Ruth bows low to the ground. "Why have I found favor in your sight that you should take notice of me, since I am a foreigner?" Boaz insists it is because he has heard of her devotion to Naomi. "May the Lord reward your work, and your wages be full from the Lord, the God of Israel, under whose wings you have come to seek refuge."

At mealtime, Boaz seeks out Ruth and asks her to share the meal. "Come here, that you may eat of the bread and dip your piece of bread in the vinegar." So Ruth sits down and Boaz serves her roasted grain. At the end of the day, Boaz orders his harvesters to "Let her glean even among the sheaves, and do not insult her. Also you shall purposely pull out for her some grain from the bundles and leave it that she may glean, and do not rebuke her."

It is obvious that Boaz is quite taken with Ruth and not only because of her devotion to Naomi. When she goes home to tell her mother-in-law all that occurred, Naomi is quick to note the light shining in Ruth's eyes at mention of Boaz. It's a perfect match thinks Naomi. Moreover Boaz is a relative and if he marries Ruth, he will fulfill the custom of the husband's relative marrying his widow to provide sons for his name

Naomi Plans a Seduction for her Daughter-in-Law

Weeks pass and Naomi thinks that it's high time for the loving couple to make it official. She realizes that Boaz may be reluctant to declare himself since there is a closer kinsman to her son Mahlon, Ruth's late husband, who has first claim on Ruth. Boaz must firmly be shown that he and Ruth are meant for each other and no one else. Naomi sits Ruth down for a talk, hoping that the girl won't be too shocked at what she is about to suggest.

"My daughter, shall I not seek security for you, that it may be well with you," security meaning marriage. And immediately Naomi brings up Boaz's name, "Now is not Boaz our kinsman with whose maids you were?" Then she points out that Boaz will be winnowing barley at the threshing floor that night, and proposes that Ruth "Wash yourself therefore, and anoint yourself and put on your best clothes, and go down to the threshing floor; but do not make yourself known to the man until he has finished eating and drinking." When he is ready to sleep, notice where he is lying "and you shall go and uncover his feet and lie down; then he will tell you what you shall do."

Ruth may be surprised but she isn't shocked, even though "feet" is a biblical euphemism for the male sex organ. Gentle she may be, but she is also a realist. If this is the only way to bring matters to a happy conclusion, then so be it. Moreover, she trusts Naomi and knows that her mother-in-law would never do anything immoral or hurtful to anyone. "All that you say I will do," Ruth agrees.

So the young woman goes down to the threshing floor and watches as Boaz finishes dinner and goes to lie down by a heap of grain. Quietly she follows, lies down next to him and begins to have second thoughts. Will Boaz think her too forward and reject her? Hours pass until finally in the middle of the night Boaz awakens and finds a woman next to him. Startled he asks who she is. Ruth answers "I am Ruth your maid. So spread your covering over your maid, for you are a close relative."

If Ruth is being even more forward by telling him to spread his covering, by mentioning his status as a relative, she is clearly telling him that it is marriage she has in mind. Far from thinking less of her Boaz is in fact delighted that she has chosen him. "May you be blessed of the Lord, my daughter. You have shown your last kindness to be better than the first by not going after young men, whether poor or rich. And he tells her "I will do for you whatever you ask, for all my people in the city know that you are a woman of excellence."

Now that they have confessed their feelings to each other, there remains only the problem of the other kinsman, but Boaz reassures Ruth that he will straighten out the situation as soon as possible and nothing will stand in the way of their marrying. Meanwhile he tells Ruth to "Lie down until morning." Then before the sun rises, Boaz protectively makes sure that Ruth leaves before anyone should recognize her.

When Ruth shares with Naomi all that has happened, Naomi is satisfied that Boaz "will not rest until he has settled it today." She is right. Boaz wastes no time in finding his kinsmen and persuading him that Ruth is not the right wife for him.

The way is clear for the couple and Naomi is overjoyed. She thought she would never know happiness again but when Ruth gives birth to a son, "Naomi takes the child and lays him in her lap, and becomes his nurse. And all of her friends proclaim that "A son has been born to Naomi!"

It is a happy ending for Naomi, Boaz and his foreign wife. God will show his approval by making Ruth's descendant, King David.

Ezra's War Against Women of the "Lands"

Four centuries after the time of Ruth (1000 BC) it was not so happy a time for the wives of those Israelites who returned from the Babylonian exile in 500 BC. Stern proclamations were issued by one of Israel's most prominent figures, Ezra, that the men must get rid of their foreign wives and their children. Who was Ezra and why was he so implacable, even cruel when it came to these women?

Ezra was a Jew who had been born in exile in Babylon, his family having been expelled from their home after the conquest of Jerusalem by the Babylonian ruler Nebuchadnezzar in 600 BC. Fifty years later, the fortunes of the Jewish community turn suddenly brighter when a remarkably enlightened ruler defeats the Babylonians and comes to power. Cyrus of Persia proves to be tolerant of different faiths and thinks it only fair that the Jews be allowed to return to their homeland and rebuild their temple if they so wished.

Ezra, "a scribe skilled in the law of Moses," leads the second of three groups of returnees. Not everyone wanted to "return," however. Many Jews were content where they were living and considered it home. Of those who did return, a number had married non-Jewish born women, much to Ezra's dismay. "When I heard about this matter, I tore my garment and my robe, and pulled some of the hair from my head and my beard, and sat down appalled."

He fears that "the holy race has intermingled with the peoples of the lands," meaning "those of the Canaanites, the Hittites, the Perizzites, the Jebusites, the Ammonites, the Moabites, the Egyptians and the Amorites."

Have any of these women accepted Yahweh as their god as Ruth did? It isn't clear. And if they haven't, does Ezra ask them to? Or does Ezra simply feel that their foreign blood is an evil contagion in itself, one that cannot be overcome even by conversion? They will surely bring in false idols and cause their husbands to "do what is evil in the sight of the Lord," the phrase repeated throughout the Bible. As for the children, they are considered as belonging to their mothers and not the responsibility of the men who sired them.

Ezra appoints leaders to investigate the matter and report the names of the miscreants. All go along with Ezra until two men, Jonathan and

Jahzeiah object. Do they themselves have foreign wives? They aren't later listed among the "guilty." Perhaps someone in their family does, or maybe they simply feel strongly that this policy is wrong. After their challenge, two more come forward to support them, Meshullam and Shabbethai. What happens to these men when they fail to sway anyone? Are they allowed to remain in the community or are they excommunicated? We aren't told.

To their Wives and Children: Go!

When the investigation is complete, the men gather along with Ezra and the list of offenders is read aloud. They come from all different segments of Jewish society; such as Eliezer of the aristocratic priestly class to Shallum the gatekeeper. What happens next? Were the wives present as well to hear, or did they remain at home, terrified at what they knew was coming.

Eliezer and Shallum would then have gone home. What do they say to their now ex-wives, to their sons and daughters? Perhaps they have determined to be stern, to keep their emotions in check and not give way to any sign of weakness such as a loving voice or a compassionate glance. They must not listen to the pleading cries of the women, or look too closely at the tear-streaked faces of their children. What do they say? Only that, you must go now, go back to your own country?

We are not told of any official provision being made for these women and children and indeed their fate seems to have been considered irrelevant. Perhaps they are given some money, some food and if they refuse to go they are driven away. One can assume that traveling through a world of limited resources many if not most faired badly. Some of them might have gotten back safely to their families in far off cities, but others no doubt would have been the victims of violence and starvation.

Ezra is considered one of Judaism's greatest figures. It is he who is supposed to have edited the various biblical writings and organized them into a true cohesive whole, the beginning of the Bible as we know it today. For the Jews, now scattered, this was the anchor they needed to help keep them together as a people.

But for Ezra, this was just a beginning. He passionately felt that his people must look inward, fearing that outside influences would prove fatal to the Jewish people as a whole. He had seen first hand what living in a foreign land had done. The Israelites had acquired different customs, spoke different languages and were used to seeing other religious practices. Ezra wanted to stamp out this otherness and bring his people back to what he saw as a state of righteousness and purity. Only in this way would the Jews survive as he believed God wanted them to. For Ezra, tolerance was a synonym for sin.

What about the story of Ruth? Did Ezra know the story of this foreign-born woman and how she accepted the god of the Hebrews and became the great grandmother of King David? We don't know. Although Ezra comes after Ruth in the course of history, the Book of Ruth may have been written down long after Ezra lived. In fact, one theory has it that the Book of Ruth was written down specifically as a counter to Ezra's decrees.

It is unfair to judge ancient peoples by today's standards. Yet during Ezra's own time, we have the example of King Cyrus and his successors, without whom the Jews would never have been allowed to return to Jerusalem, rebuild their temple and practice their faith. It was Cyrus' enlightened attitude toward other peoples, religions and customs that enables Ezra to do his life's work of editing the five books of Moses and codifying the laws. It is sad that Ezra did not feel he could afford to extend that same generosity of spirit towards those nameless women and children.

TO THE READER: AN AFTERWARD AS FOREWORD

It has been a joy writing this little book. And I hope that you the reader have enjoyed at least parts of it, and have found yet other parts which have stimulated your own thinking about the Bible, and perhaps have even touched your present life as well. There is no final word on such matters. We help each other interpret and re-interpret as we move along.

I am now working on a second small volume, a follow-up to this one. It will focus more on the question of God's own evolution - as aided and abetted by humankind's evolution (for God best sees himself through humankind). It is my firm opinion that God and humans have evolved together. We are co-conspirators in this great adventure. That is the great responsibility that lies on both of us as we continue to grow.

Just as humankind is evolving in a sort of stutter-step dance (two steps forward, one step back), so God is also moving forward on his rhythmic journey. It is a bumpy road for both of us.

On the following page is a brief Table of Contents for my next volume. This will be followed by a third and concluding volume, which will contain a sum-up.

Thank you again for "listening" to me: listening isn't a free gift, so I thank you for it.

PREVIEW OF THE NEXT VOLUME OF "DOES GOD EVOLVE"?

Forthcoming Volume 2

Progress (and Regress): God Moves in Mysterious Ways

I. Primitive Origin: God as Angry Father & Ruthless Tribal Chieftain – Conquest, Revenge, and Booty
   • God murders all first-born Egyptian children (Exodus 12:29)
   • Joshua annihilates all men, women, and babies--even animals--in the cities of Jericho, Ai, and Hazor (Joshua 6)
   • God orders Moses to divide up 32,000 captured virgins as soldier's pay for Holy War (Numbers 31:35)
   • God says Jews should sacrifice their first-born sons to him (unless they pay a fee) (Exodus 13)
   • God has a Jewish tribe wipe out another Jewish tribe, except for 400 virgins (Judges 21:11)

II. Initial Progress: God descends from His Mountain to Discuss a Few Things with Mankind
   • God debates with Abraham: Are there ten good men in Sodom? (Genesis 18:32)
   • God debates with Moses: When one man sins, why should one destroy the entire community? (Numbers 16:22)
   • God discusses the creation of the hoarfrost and the Pleiades with Job (Job 38:29, 38:31)
   • God is conflicted about awarding humans the gift of inquiry and curiosity (Tree of Knowledge)
   • God teaches Abraham to discontinue child sacrifice (Genesis 22:12)

III. Some Backsliding
   • God consents to the human sacrifice of Jephthah's daughter (Judges 11:30)
   • God, in tribe-mind fashion, murders the sons of the sinner instead of the sinner himself (Ahab, see I Kings 21:29)
   • Ezra orders all Jewish men to cast out their 'foreign' wives and children into the desert (Ezra 10:3)

IV. Progress: God Evolves toward Tolerance
   • God preaches tolerance to Jonah, a narrow-minded prophet

• The overlooked parable of God's "Saint" Esau

• God's prophet Micah scorns those who think God wants them to sacrifice their firstborn sons for their sins (Micah 6:7).

• God's messengers Amos and Micah: perform actual good deeds, not just religious rituals at temple (Amos 5:21, Micah 6)

• God reminds the Jews that he cares about other nations as well: "I think as much of the Black people of Ethiopia in Africa as I do of you. And, just as I helped you out of Egypt, I helped the Philistines out of Crete, the Syrians out of Kir (Amos 9:7)

• God has Jesus and his brother James follow in the footsteps of Amos and Micah: faith without deeds is an empty faith (James 2:17)

V. Toward a God of Love, Kindness, Good Deeds, and Animal Rights

• By day God directs his love and kindness to me, by night his song is with me (Psalm 42:8)

• Justice should be impartial, 'blindfolded:' treat both rich and poor equally before the Law (Exodus 23:3)

• Do not punish children for the sins of their parents. We are each individually responsible for our acts (Ezekiel 18:19)

• Do not spread false rumors about others (Exodus 23:1)

• Don't follow a crowd to do evil (Exodus 23:2)

• Animal rights: Balaam's donkey questions him: "Why are you beating me, sir?" (Numbers 22:28)

VI. Summary: God needs us as much as we need Him

ABOUT THE AUTHOR

Lori Miles is a firm believer that God does not punish people because they attend a certain house of worship. God is big enough to accept different people with diverse rituals and varying beliefs. He can even accept atheists.

Ms. Miles is not only a lover of the Bible but also a lover of history—particularly of the periods of the Renaissance and the Reformation. She also likes to swing dance, and takes very seriously Ecclesiastes' advice that "there is a season for every activity under the heavens" and that there is indeed "a time to dance."

BACK COVER

Bible Stories You've Never Heard Before

Through close readings of overlooked tales and new angles on well-known ones, Lori Miles opens up paths through the Bible that you've never seen before.

Uncovering the tracks of the Divine, she probes deeply into God's statements and silences, revealing a gripping saga of oscillating progressions and regressions, in such stories as:
- The Garden of Eden and the Curiosity Tree
- The magic chest, surmounted by two golden statues of angels, and a seat for God to sit on
- Esau as overlooked First Saint in the Bible

Weaving her magical way through back roads and undiscovered trails in the Good Book, Miles also champions those down-and-out creatures who have normally lived only on the margins of our consciousness:
- Hagar and her young son Ishmael, cast out from Abraham's tent onto the vast nothingness of the barren desert
- That Much-Maligned Caller-Up-of-the-Dead, the Witch of Endor
- King David's long-suffering wife Michal--who is "married to the mob"

Traversing biblical landscapes and seeking out the shifting lairs of the divine, Miles opens up a world with stubbornness, tragedy, and even humor. Her sum-up: "God needs us as much as we need Him; I think God is looking for a new kind of covenant with us."

After diving into these fresh pages, you will never read the Bible with quite the same eyes again.

www.ingramcontent.com/pod-product-compliance
Lightning Source LLC
Chambersburg PA
CBHW071419040426
42331CB00050B/2512